THEY SNATCHED MY PLAYGROUND

KHALID JEHANGIR

Vitasta
LET KNOWLEDGE SPREAD

Published by
Renu Kaul Verma
Vitasta Publishing Pvt Ltd
2/15, Ansari Road, Daryaganj
New Delhi - 110 002
info@vitastapublishing.com

ISBN 978-93-86473-67-7

First Edition 2019
MRP ₹ 495

Cover and layout by Somesh Kumar Mishra
Printed by Vikas Computer and Printers

Contents

Acknowledgements

I thank my late dear father Sheikh Ghulam Mohammad for imbibing in me the values that make me a Kashmiri. Honestly, these values have helped me all my life. I could feel his gentle and loving presence around me as I was conceptualising and writing this book. I am proud to say that I have inherited his faith in syncretism and I proudly uphold his belief that future of the people of Kashmir is safe with India.

I also owe my gratitude to former Vice Chancellor of Kashmir University Dr Riyaz Punjabi and senior journalist Aasha Khosa for their guidance for this book.

I am grateful to all my colleagues and friends in India and the USA for their unrelenting support.

I will remain eternally grateful to my alma mater, Burn Hall School, for its motto: "Industria Floremus" (In toil we shall flourish), which has always been the guiding principle of my life.

I owe loads of gratitude to my beloved wife Susan Khalid for her patience and perseverance. She took charge of everything that I couldn't attend to due to my public life and the writing of this book for nearly one year.

Preface

I was quite lucky to have been born at a time when Kashmir was like no other place on this planet. The land was resplendent with gardens and flowers and the mighty Chinars that blazed in rusty hues before their leaves dropped off for the winter season; meandering rivers and gushing waterfalls, cool breeze that was balmy and a harsh winter that seemed to be Nature's way of humbling the people of this land. We were blessed to live in neighbourhoods where the sounds of *azan* and *aarti* blended to fill the air with a divine melody. My childhood belief was that all Kashmiris—Hindus, Muslims, Sikhs and others—are one people.

Alas, this didn't last long! As I was about to enter my adolescence, the gun had arrived in my land. A few young boys were misled into believing in a cause worth picking up guns for; they were taken to Pakistan, fed poisonous thoughts and sent back with Kalashnikovs, grenades and rocket launchers for carrying out *jihad*.

I was growing up seeing my neighbourhood break up. Hindus left Kashmir to escape violence and mayhem. In spite of being erudite and famously farsighted Kashmiris, the Pandits had no idea that their exile would not end soon. Most of them had left their homes in a hurry believing they would return within months as the law and order situation would improve. Muslims too believed that the armed rebellion staged by a few boys was unsustainable and would fade away soon. Three decades later, Kashmiri Pandits continue to live with a sense of betrayal and yearning to return while Muslims continue to face the worst and unimaginable sufferings. Every day, coffins of young men are being lowered into the soil in some corner of the Valley. Thousands of families are living in grief and penury after losing their sole breadwinners to terrorism.

The Valley remains swathed in melancholy and grief.

I feel angry at the few men who had picked up the gun. One generation of Kashmiris has faced the dreadful consequences of their misdemeanour. In fact, my generation faced a Tsunami of violence and disturbances while the next generation is facing an uncertain future as they don't even know what normal life is.

I have always believed that life is a gift. We must live it to the fullest and our aim should not be to get into our grave at the earliest, whatever the cause.

In Kashmir, the young are made to court death because merchants of death are everywhere. They are guiding them to their graves; there is nobody to tell them how to make the best of their life. Nobody tells the young Kashmiris that by firing at a security person on duty they would not get *azadi*; it would lead to retaliation and more deaths. Nobody tells them that picking up the gun and shooting people is not *jihad*. What use is the utopian *azadi* if they are not alive to see it—somebody has to tell them.

No wonder young men in their teens are today joining terrorist groups; they seem to be born with a death wish. *Mujhe to shaheed hona hai*, is the catchphrase among the young boys of the present generation. Death has become a romantic notion for them.

The merchants of death include politicians, separatists, Pakistan's Kashmir managers, propagandists, religious leaders etc. Interestingly, the Hurriyat Conference leaders, who are clearly on the side of Pakistan, glorify the dead militants while taking great care to ensure safety and a good life for their children. The Hurriyat and other separatists have emerged as a new elite club in Kashmir. They are trying to replace a set of oligarchs like the Abdullah and the Mufti families. Most of the separatist leaders flaunt their newly acquired wealth; almost all have sent their children away for education. Their children become doctors, engineers, bureaucrats and some manage to grab cushy government jobs with or without merit while their fathers make speeches exhorting the youth to take up the gun. Their frequent call for *hartal* creates an ambience of doom and gloom. Living a normal life is almost impossible in Kashmir.

My generation of Kashmiris is angry at New Delhi, for it has always reposed far greater trust in a few families than common people. The favourites are the Abdullahs—the progeny of Sheikh Mohammad Abdullah—and the Muftis, scions of Mufti Mohammad Saeed, first Kashmiri Home Minister of India. These families manipulate New Delhi into believing that unless they are installed in power, Kashmir will go to Pakistan. This is how the generations of Abdullahs and the Muftis rose to power making people angry.

Pakistan too toed the same line; it patronised the Geelanis and Mirwaiz family in furthering its narrative and cause in Kashmir.

The youth of my generation grew up amidst chilling stories of abductions, killings, massacres and encounters. One does not need a psychologist to explain how traumatic all this is for a young person. To add to their fears, suddenly the cities and towns changed into a fortress, with mud bunkers manned by security forces erupting everywhere. We felt stifled and imprisoned. We could no longer roam around aimlessly in gay abandon. The gun had also killed our youthful spirit. Our minds were full of fears—of death caused by a bullet or shrapnel of a grenade—and our dreams were dead.

That was the world of what I call the mid-militancy generation.

At forty-two today, as I take baby steps in my journey into public life and move towards middle age, I want to tell the story of my generation to the world. Obviously, I am not old and experienced enough to write an autobiography.

I have tried to paint a canvas of Kashmir where I was growing up. I speak for myself and a silent majority of people of my generation who have missed the happiness and joys of growing up in a normal world and yet are eternally optimistic.

Childhood Lost

Winter is a dull time in Kashmir; the sun remains hidden behind a thick amalgam of smog and clouds and trees turn into silhouettes of bare branches. The countryside landscape turns into a brown expanse of fallow land. However, nothing comes in the way of spirited young boys playing cricket, a sub-continental sports staple, even in this smudgy landscape. I always looked forward to my winter break from school in Srinagar to play cricket with friends in my ancestral town of Ganderbal in central Kashmir.

Every morning after breakfast, my friends and I would get together at Qamriya playground, located close to the shrine of Sufi Saint Qamriya sahib. In fact, the ground was a favourite haunt of the young townsfolk of all ages. After warming up we would play a passionate game until noon. Thereafter, we would count each minute waiting for the messenger sent by our mothers to call us for lunch. I clearly remember that particular day when darkness seemed to have descended on us. It was a cold December day; the game was in full swing and suddenly we saw a phiren-clad stranger rushing towards the pitch. Almost hysterical, he broke the news, "Maulana Masoodi has been shot dead!"

The news left us stunned; we stopped the game. Though many of us had not seen Maulana Masoodi in person, most of us knew that he was a veteran leader who had played an important role in shaping Kashmir's history. I knew that he was old and frail and remained mostly inside his house.

Why would someone kill an 87-year old bedridden man? I thought.

Unlike most other political leaders who lived in palatial houses and moved around with trappings of power and authority, Maulana Masoodi lived in a small single-storey house, located on the banks of River Sind in village Dauderhama, just on the outskirts of Ganderbal. Everyone respected him for his honesty, integrity and religious scholarship and people looked up to him for blessings and advice. However, strangely, younger generations of Kashmiris never get to learn about stalwarts like him in school and, therefore, many of us are in no position to appreciate their role. I had heard about him from elders at home; from my grandfather and my father. Everybody showed reverence towards him and explained to me that Maulana sahib had played a significant role in the events that led to the state of Jammu and Kashmir joining India and not Pakistan in 1947. Later on, he never hankered after official positions or money and lived a simple life. These briefings at home had created an image of a *Dervesh* (ascetic) in my mind. In my thoughts, Maulana sahib was a godly man who worked for humanity. He was also great because of his simplicity and detachment from power politics.

That morning, a young Kashmiri, maybe my age or a little older, had entered the Masoodi house. Back then, in Kashmir, nobody dared to stop a stranger, more so a young boy, from entering one's house. Arguing with strangers was dangerous since nobody knew how to tell a militant, who may flash his pistol from under his phiren any time, from an innocent boy of the neighbourhood. Everyone played safe.

The intruder demanded to see Maulana sahib. He was ushered into his room by one of the women members of the family. Maulana sahib was almost bedridden and spent all his time inside his room. The intruder must have looked angry. He apparently entered Maulana's room and addressed him in a raised voice, "Maulana! Don't you feel ashamed for having supported Jammu and Kashmir's accession with the Indian Union? You should apologise for this shameful act?" Maulana replied in a feeble voice, *"I did what I thought was right, you do what you think is right."* The stranger fired three bullets from his pistol at the old man. The bullets hit his frail chest.

When other members of the Masoodi household heard the sound of gunshots they rushed to his room. There the old man lay in a pool of blood that was gushing out from his chest as he took his last breath. The assassin had fired from a close range, obviously to make sure the old man had no chance to survive.

The incident shattered me. I kept thinking why a Kashmiri would kill a fellow countryman in cold blood—why would anyone kill a man who was old, infirm, inactive, and in all probability was not going to live very long? The townsfolk were privately grieving Maulana's tragic end. However, his funeral was a small affair attended by his family as neighbours and other townsfolk were too scared to show solidarity with them. Even though I was too young to gauge the public mood, I clearly remember I felt deeply depressed for days together.

To me, Maulana sahib was a relic of an era when the Indian subcontinent was going through the partition. Pakistan was becoming a new country amidst bloodshed and hate of an unprecedented level. As a child, I had always believed that it was better for me to be living in India than in Pakistan. I also knew that it was due to the efforts of leaders like Maulana Masoodi and Sheikh Mohammad Abdullah that I was an Indian and not a Pakistani. I was also conscious that in India, Hindus, Muslims, and people of so many other religions live together while Pakistan was a land of Muslims only. I always believed Maulana had taken the right decision for the people of Kashmir.

Maulana's death had petrified the people across Ganderbal. The general refrain was that Maulana's killer was a *Jamaiti*, a term loosely used to refer to a member of Jamait-e-Islami, an Islamic organisation. However, of late, this term is being used loosely to refer to anyone with a hard-line approach to Islam.

Next day, Maulana's killers were brazenly celebrating his death. Newspapers—published from Srinagar and Jammu in Urdu and English—carried a small report about the veteran's murder, hardly befitting his stature. However, the same newspapers had published—in detail—the statement of the chief of Hizbullah militant outfit Saiful Islam (ref....*Kashmir: Under siege* A G Noorani) on the killing. Saiful Islam was his code name as a gun-wielding militant; nobody knew his real name. He boisterously admitted that his group was behind Maulana's killing.

According to his statement, 'Maulana Masoodi's life was full of black acts' and he was one of the most dreaded 'traitors' and 'betrayers' of Islam. The order for his murder was issued in consultation with ulemas (Islamic scholars). Islam had the temerity to release a charge-sheet against the Maulana. The charges included his support for secularism as against Islam; taking Kashmir closer to India. Masoodi was the brain behind rechristening Muslim Conference, the political party founded by Sheikh Mohammad Abdullah, as a more secular sounding National Conference. It had happened in 1939 and yet Islam held it against him. Maulana Masoodi was also presumed guilty of helping India push back the raiders who had been sent by Pakistan to liberate Kashmir in October 1947. Interestingly, these raiders comprised tribesmen and Pak army regulars from North-West Frontier Province who had looted and burnt properties, ransacked places of worship and even raped women across North Kashmir before the Army landed in Srinagar. They had harmed Kashmiris in all possible ways and left deep scars on their minds. A popular slogan, *Pakistanas dakistaan* (let Pakistan be damned) emerged those days; it could be heard during years of insurgency whenever people faced violence from terrorists who flaunted their affiliation to Pakistan. It was used quite often in private conversations. Saiful Islam claimed that in 1965, the Maulana had informed the Indian authorities about the presence of a secret army of Islamic mujahideen who had sneaked into Kashmir to 'liberate' the land for Pakistan and got them arrested.

Islam had declared Maulana guilty on all these counts and ordered his execution! Kangaroo courts with summary justice had almost become a way of life in Kashmir's hinterland.

Hizbullah chief's statement also served a warning to other 'traitors'. He claimed to have prepared a list of 'traitors' and warned that they would meet the same fate as Maulana Masoodi. The message sent a chill down every Kashmiri's spine. I felt very unsafe in Ganderbal; I didn't agree with the views of Hizbullah. I could never imagine such a towering and saintly person being called names like 'traitor'.

Playing cricket in Qamriya was never the same again; I would always be conscious of my surroundings. Who knew someone may be coming to break the news of another murder anytime on the pitch.

Within a few months, the annual cricket tournament was organised in Qamriya cricket ground. After the finals, the organisers had invited Ghulam Ahmed Saloora, head of the youth wing of National Conference, for distribution of awards. The moment his name was announced as chief guest, some youth owing allegiance to the Jamait created commotion; they raised slogans to insult the guest and against India. Saloora, who was given the nickname of 'Aame Youth' (Aame for Ahmed and Youth for his party) beat a hasty retreat. The incident was a clear signal that the Jamaiti-types were always ready to wrest the ground from the common people of Kashmir.

Cricket was the rage with Kashmiri youth; Qamriya was

also known as cricket ground. After this incident our parents strictly warned us against venturing out and especially forbade us from visiting Qamriya again. Soon, gunmen owing allegiance to Jamat-e-islami had taken control of the cricket ground. There, they would practise gun shooting. On August 14, the independence day of Pakistan, they organised a 'military' parade at Qamriya. In that ceremony, the gunmen wearing fake battle fatigues saluted the Pakistani flag and offered it a gun salute. We, the former players, were asked to fill the spectators stands. I remember, the first time I watched the parade I was emotionless; I could never make sense of anything. Probably my mind was full of resentment for the perceived involvement of the Jamait-e-Islami in the killing of Maulana Sahib. I watched in trepidation how they had snatched my playground and turned it into a canvas to paint it with their ideology.

Their military might, gun display, and the ceremonial march past left me cold.

Later, when the Army took control of the situation, the Qamriya ground was used for assembling townsfolk during the Cordon And Search Operations (CASO). The exercise would involve soldiers or policemen making an early morning cordon of a large *mohalla*. People would be woken up from their sleep through the announcement from mega phones of loud speakers. They would be asked to assemble at Qamriya ground. The troops, in the meanwhile, conducted a door-to-door search for arms and ammunition. Often the search would be a follow up of precise information. Often an informer, whose face would remain covered by a mask, would accompany the troops. Everyone would fear the masked man the most. His one nod for a man passing in front of the gypsy van in which he himself would be sitting behind a mesh-covered windshield would send him to a virtual hell. He could tell an innocent from a terrorist. Though the informers often told the truth, even the innocents feared that the masked man was their enemy or rival and would use his power to settle old scores.

The exercise caused a lot of inconvenience to people; yet it also led to arrests of terrorists and unearthing of arms and ammunition dumps. I thought it was like a medicine, which is often a bitter pill that one has to swallow to get cured of a disease.

My friend and I were dejected at losing our Qamriya playground.

However, my parents were lucky to have witnessed the glorious phase of Qamriya. In early eighties, they had seen the shooting of Bollywood film *Silsila* featuring Amitabh Bachchan, Rekha and Jaya Bachchan in this ground. A popular song *Yeh kahan aa gaye hum…* from the movie shot on the Big B and Rekha has the magnificent Chinars of Qamriya as the backdrop in many scenes.

Today, the Chinars of Qamriya continue to stand tall as mute witnesses to the changing times of Kashmir.

Being Indian

India and Pakistan fought a thirteen-day war in December 1971. The war ended decisively with Pakistan's division—its eastern part became Bangladesh—and also shattered the myth of religion being the basis of a viable nation. Pakistan, the land of the pure—as its founders visualised it—was created for Muslims. However, within twenty-five years, its 6.6 crore Bengali-speaking people had risen in revolt. The Bengali-speaking Pakistanis could never understand why Urdu, a hybrid language, was being imposed on them. They were a majority in Pakistan and since Bengali was an ancient language with its rich literature, art and music traditions, they expected Bengali to be Pakistan's official language. The Bengalis could never reconcile to this harsh reality in Pakistan. Gradually, they faced brazen discrimination and indignities heaped on them by their western Muslim compatriots. In 1969, Sheikh

Mujibur Rahman, the Bengali-speaking leader of the Awami League won the general elections and yet he was not allowed to become the prime minister. This proved to be the last nail in the coffin of Bengalis' patience.

When the Bengalis revolted, Islamabad reacted by sending in its Army to put down the revolt. The Army resorted to a reign of repression—rapes, killings, massacres and arson—forcing 10 million Bengalis to seek shelter in refugee camps in India. At the end, New Delhi had to intervene militarily. In the ensuing war, the Pakistani army faced a humiliating defeat and Bangladesh was born as a free country.

I was born four-and-a-half years later, on June 30, 1976, in Srinagar as the youngest of the three children of Sheikh Ghulam Mohammad and Misra Begum. As a child, I grew up realising that my father had played an important role in the 1971 war. He was posted in the Procurement (Defence) Department of the state government that works with the Indian Army in far flung areas and border districts. The department is administratively part of the State government and is funded by the Ministry of Defense. My father's job was to ensure supplies of arms, ammunition, food, rations and even salaries to the soldiers posted on the border. Back then Kashmir had scanty road network and, therefore, ensuring supplies to the frontiers was a huge responsibility. During the war, my father was in charge of Chowkibal and Uri in the snowbound mountains of North Kashmir. At the end of the war, he was awarded a commendation certificate by the Army Chief and a medal of the Dogra regiment for his services. The framed certificate and the medal were displayed in the wooden showcase in the drawing room of our house.

I would lose no opportunity to pick up the medal and caress it. It gave me a surge of energy and pride and maybe evoked my love for my father, who would mostly remain out of Srinagar for work and visit us on some weekends. I was particularly fascinated by the image of two tigers, the insignia of the Dogra Regiment, on the medal. As I kept it back in the showcase, I would feel overwhelmed by the thought that my father was an extraordinary man.

We lived in a four-bedroom house in Jawahar Nagar, a predominantly Hindu neighbourhood; it was allotted to my father by the government. Early morning, besides *azan* from the mosques, I would get to hear *bhajans* and *aarti* from the temples. However, as a child, I always looked forward to the family's visits to our ancestral home in Ganderbal. The Sheikh family owned an 18-bedroom mansion and my grandparents lived there. Our house was in a 24-kanal orchard of apples and walnuts and it had a panoramic view of the milky white Sind River that came cascading from Ladakh and meandered through the plains of the Valley to merge with the Jhelum. Close by was the shrine of Sufi saint Qamar Sahib that I loved to visit.

Standing on the banks of Sind, I always felt refreshed; my mind got soaked in the bliss of something divine.

FAMILY HISTORY

The Sheikhs of Ganderbal were *jagirdars* who owned large swathes of land. Another interesting story about our family was that we were among the last of the Hindus to adopt Islam. In fact, in Kashmir many Muslims can easily trace their Hindu ancestors. The Sheikhs were Kashmiri Brahmins who had changed their religion to Islam. Though we were landlords, our family was just well-to-do and not rich, as many outside believed. Some of my cousins and uncles had ventured into business while others took up jobs. However, the most famous person of our family so far remains my father's cousin, Ghulam Qadir *Ganderbali*, who we called *Qadir toth* (Qadir, the dear one in Kashmiri). He was the first Indian Police Service (IPS) officer of Jammu and Kashmir. A man of integrity and courage, Ganderbali, was a staunch and vocal supporter of Kashmir's accession to India. He would quote the rule book and the Constitution of J&K to make the point that J&K is an inalienable part of India. As chief of the police force, he felt it was his responsibility to uphold the Constitution and the status of Kashmir. In fact, he was for total integration of Jammu and Kashmir with the Indian domain and was famously intolerant of those who tried to broker a debate on the finality of the accession. *Qadir toth* always defended his stance saying that as a policeman he would have to go by the rule book and the law. Nobody ever won an argument with him.

No wonder, when it came to arresting the then *Wazir-e-azam* (prime minister) Sheikh Mohammad Abdullah in 1958, who, the Nehru government in Delhi suspected was in the middle of hatching a conspiracy to break Kashmir from India, Ganderbali was handpicked for the job. His conscience was clear; anyone working against the Constitution needed to be dealt with by the law of the land. So he went to Sheikh Abdullah and arrested him. Considering that Sheikh Abdullah was indeed the most popular leader at that time, Ganderbali's was, indeed, a bold act. Later, my uncle became an important authority in

Ghulam Mohammad Bakshi's government that launched a massive developmental drive in Jammu and Kashmir. Many of the landmark buildings and roads in Srinagar came up during his regime. Ganderbali dealt with pro-Pakistani elements and secessionists, some of whom had emerged under the banner of Plebiscite Front, with an iron hand.

Sheikh Abdullah's supporters, many of them members of the Plebiscite Front, spread canards against Ganderbali and our family calling us 'traitors'. After Sheikh's arrest, Pakistan Radio had upped its propaganda on Kashmir. Many people in Kashmir listened to it, some even believed its brazen lies but in the Sheikh household, it was proscribed.

Our family firmly believed in the idea of inclusive and secular India as against that of Pakistan which was based on religion. The lives and thoughts of Mahatma Gandhi and Pandit Jawahar Lal Nehru inspired my father and his brothers. Sheikh Mohammad Abdullah had also believed in the same philosophy. The beliefs of my father and his brother faced a test in the autumn of 1947. Maharaja Hari Singh was indecisive on making a choice. He had offered a standstill agreement to India and Pakistan. He had asked for some time so that he could make a clear choice.

However, while the Maharaja was still thinking, in the third week of October, the Pakistan Army launched a covert operation to wrest Kashmir. The soldiers, accompanied by 6,000 tribesmen from North-West Frontier Province (since renamed as Khyber Pakhtunwa), attacked Kashmir. They had already taken control of Muzaffarabad town and what is today Pakistan occupied Kashmir and entered Kashmir via Uri.

On October 18, the tribesmen had entered Baramulla where they indulged in an orgy of loot, rape and killings. On October 23rd, on Maharaja Hari Singh's appeal and his decision to sign the document of accession, the Indian Army was flown to Kashmir. The Army quickly repelled the attackers who were closing in on Srinagar and the airport. A battle was fought at Shalteng, the entry point to Srinagar from the north. The attack was repulsed but many of the raiders had taken shelter in the homes of their local sympathisers. My father and his brothers worked quietly to extract information about these *Kabalis* (tribals) and informed the Army. They were also involved in the civil defense force that was raised of volunteers. The men and women of the civil defense force displayed wooden guns over their shoulders and marched in Srinagar and many towns shouting slogans like *Khabardaar aiy hamlawar; hum kashmiri hain tayyar* (Beware the attackers, we, the Kashmiris, are ready to take you on). Their presence was meant to instill a sense of security in the minds of general public, as people were panicky after hearing stories of *kabalis*' savagery in Baramulla. My father had quietly contacted many Indian missions abroad informing them about the ground realities so that the envoys could disseminate correct information to the world in the face of massive Pakistani propaganda. I often marvel at his commitment and capacity to accomplish such a big task at a time when there was no social media, internet, and even telephone was a luxury.

Ganderbali was like his brothers but made of even sterner stuff. He carried the reputation of being an unwavering nationalist who suppressed anti-national elements that had started raising their heads soon after Sheikh's dismissal and his arrest in 1953, with an iron hand.

However, *Qadir toth's* reputation was a mixed bag for our family. Loyalty to our country was non-negotiable for all of us. However, for his detractors, Ganderbali and his family were 'pariahs'. Many of his critics conveniently chose to ignore the fact that my uncle had remained loyal to Sheikh Abdullah, the prime minister. It was after he showed signs of being unsure on the finality of the accession, that Ganderbali had no moral dilemma in treating him as an enemy of the State.

However, with the advent of the gun and militancy on the Kashmir scene, Ganderbali's and my father's reputation as nationalists came in handy. Ours was the only house in the town where the Army or the Security force personnel had never entered in search of lurking militants or their hidden cache of arms. I remember an afternoon when a young army officer, Brigadier Shivrein, came to our home in Ganderbal. My father had retired from service when Shivrein came on a posting in the area. As soon he entered the room and saw my father, he saluted him. I carried the tray with lemon tea for the guest and also served him and my father. As the Brigadier and my father were talking, I sat nearby just observing them. Honestly, I was in awe of the visitor who never changed his reverential tone while discussing the ground situation with my father, whom he was addressing either as 'Sir' or 'Sheikh Sahib'. My father told him categorically that he should feel free to search our house in case he ever gets information about terrorists having taken shelter there. The Brigadier smiled and told him, "Even if ten terrorists enter your house, we will never enter here. We have other ways of arresting them."

He again saluted my father before taking leave.

The incident left a deep mark on my mind. I had just seen that the Army was not only protecting us but also treating us with so much reverence and dignity. They treat us as their own, I told myself. Henceforth, I would never believe stories about how cruel the Army was. I knew it was part of the propaganda and that I should only believe what I see.

In 1975, Sheikh Mohammad Abdullah made peace with Prime Minister Indira Gandhi and became chief minister of the State. Now the National Conference wanted to take revenge on our family; the only way it could do so was to make attempts to keep us out of government jobs and positions. They were not always successful. Some of my cousins joined the government and attained top positions by sheer dint of merit and hard work. Even Qadir toth's sons are today in good positions in the State government.

However, as a boy I had been called a 'traitor' by some of my playmates who apparently had heard stories about our family and our political commitment from their parents. The National Conference activists were unsure of their nationalism; probably some of them were living in the wrong country and they had realised it a bit late in their lives. Such elements tried to spread propaganda and socially ostracise us.

Another interesting visual from our Ganderbal mansion in my mind is that of the two huge portraits of two great Kashmiris, Pandit Jawahar Lal Nehru and Bakshi Ghulam Mohammad. The portraits in oil adorned the wall of my father's bedroom. These were done by artist Azmat Rampuri in 1952 and my father had purchased these from him sometime later. During the years of insurgency when people around were scared to identify with Indian symbols and icons fearing reprisals from terrorists and their supporters, my uncles and cousins asked my father to remove the two portraits. As always, my father was clear, "Let them kill us; there is no bravery in hiding the paintings," he said with his characteristic firmness of a *fauji*. No wonder the portraits were removed only after my father passed away in 2011.

One of my cousins removed the paintings to his room.

Growing Up In Fear

Fr Dominic, the principal of Burn Hall School, Srinagar, was a man of few words. So, whenever he decided to speak in the morning assembly, we, the students, knew that he would have something substantive to say. Not that we always understood the gravity of his remarks but all students had tremendous faith in the priest from Goa. Once again, that day, we didn't catch the concerns he flagged in his terse message.

I was studying in the seventh standard. For me, my school run by Catholic priests, was the best place in the world. We played sports, attended classes and had loads of fun preparing for competitions in debates and cultural events. There was never a dull moment in my life in the school; family friends and relatives looked at me with admiration after knowing that I was a student of Burn Hall School.

My school was established by Mill Hill Fathers, a group of missionaries from Britain, in 1930. Later in 1948, they also set up Burn Hall School in Abbottabad, Pakistan. While the Srinagar school remains a prestigious institution, the one in Abbottabad has since been taken over by the Army and rechristened as Burn Hall Army School.

However, on that day, I could see deep worry lines on Father's grim face. He, perhaps for the first time, took a meaningful pause before addressing the morning assembly. He told us that the situation in Kashmir was turning serious. He made a prophetic statement: Kashmir would never be peaceful again.

After Assembly, we dismissed Father's talk as the usual grim talk that adults are good at throwing at children probably to make them become serious with studies and be disciplined. I never believed that my world of fun and happiness would ever change. Little did I know that in coming days, months and years, Father Dominic's words—Kashmir will never have peace again—would echo in my mind every day.

In hindsight, I feel there were nascent signs of the unrest around me; perhaps my nimble mind failed to read these. Some of my friends and classmates would boast of their young cousins and neighbours who had gone to Pakistan 'for training' and returned with guns and grenades to fight India. I could visualise a fight that was happening in a far-off place, maybe on a cinema screen in a Hindi film or a Hollywood flick. The imagery had no bloodletting, just a bold villain firing shots and being kicked on his ass by the hero. The villain would do a somersault before flying in the air and passing out on the ground under the impact of the hero's punch. Blood and gore was not part of Kashmiri children's imagination back then. I also thought what would people do with guns and bombs in Kashmir, the most peaceful land in the world?

One day, I heard of Sher Khan, leader of a group of men who called themselves 'Allah Tigers'. Everyone in school discussed his exploits—his threats to liquor shops and bar owners against selling alcohol. He said the intoxicating spirits was *haram* (forbidden) in Islam. One day, newspaper reports said that Khan and his army of guerillas had entered the Centaur Hotel and vandalised its bar. The hotel located on the banks of Dal Lake was a rather plain grey building, yet boasted of good services and a nice view of the lake. Many foreign tourists and officials stayed there. To me, Sher Khan looked more like a Rambo straight out of a movie; a kind of funny and not a dangerous man.

One day, while my father was driving the car and we were passing through Srinagar's Boulevard Road, I was struck by the unusual scenario—the picturesque road rimming the Dal lake was nearly deserted. I had always seen the Boulevard teeming with people—locals, young couples, families, foreigners, mobile food joints, shikarawallas, taxi drivers etc. Just the other day, they were there and now had simply vanished. My father spoke to some boatmen and they told him that after Sher Khan's well-publicised acts of vandalism, tourists feared getting caught in the violence, and had left in hordes. A pall of gloom had descended on Dal Lake area; colourful Shikaras remained leisurely parked on the ghats and people like small handicraft sellers, shawl-sellers, shikara owners, houseboat owners, petty traders who lived off tourists looked sad and depressed. The air around Dal Lake was unbearably heavy with tension and melancholy.

In the coming days, one could routinely hear the sound of explosions in Srinagar. Since blasts were happening every day, people stopped getting perturbed over those happening at a distance provided all members of their family were safe. One day, a huge blast ripped apart Srinagar city's central area of Lal Chowk. The place is hardly half a kilometer from our school. We heard the sound of the blast in our classroom. Later, we came to know that a number of passers-by had died and many got injured. Srinagar was very tense and yet, a teenager like me was not able to fully comprehend the full meaning of events happening around.

In the school, I suddenly noticed that Hindu boys had started missing school. Every Monday during the assembly we found a few boys were absent. Our teachers first ignored this development but later started marking them absent. Within three weeks almost all Hindu boys had gone away. Kashmir was becoming a dangerous place for all. The minority Hindus were the target of terror groups—many were served threats, some saw their names in the soon-to-be-executed persons list stuck on the walls of their houses by unknown persons in the night. The community was terrified after some prominent members like judges, Intelligence offices and leaders were killed in broad daylight. For the Kashmiri Pandits, the writing on the wall was clear; they left their home, hearth and everything in the Valley to escape the violence.

Our school was badly affected by the exodus of Pandit

teachers. Each time our class teacher started the roll call my heart would skip a beat when she called the names of Hindu students. A meaningful silence would fall over the classroom when they didn't answer. She would mark them absent since all of them had left in a hurry without taking a proper discharge certificate from the school.

One day in the early nineties, Father Dominic announced that the National anthem *Jana gana mana* would not be sung or played by the band in the school. He even banned the singing of *Sare jahan se accha Hindustan hamara* (India is the best in the entire world) written by a Kashmiri, Allama Iqbal, who, years after writing this beautiful paean to Mother India, had floated the idea of Pakistan. Father's order came after the terrorist outfits had issued general threats—through newspapers, posters and even letters sent to institutions—against eulogising India. *Sare jahan se* is a very inspiring song and we would sing it spiritedly in the morning assembly.

It was becoming clear that the gun had come to stay in Kashmir. Our parents forbade us from venturing out or going to the playground since no place was safe. During the recess in the school, students would get into a huddle to listen to the exploits of militants—I had no idea how much was the truth and how much hearsay and exaggeration. Soon, I realised that many of my classmates were sympathetic to and supported the cause of militants. One day, there was a whisper campaign about one of our classmates carrying a grenade in his schoolbag. I too badly wanted to see a grenade. As soon as the lunch break was announced, we all huddled around this boy. He took out the olive ball from his school bag. As he was boisterously displaying it to the curious gang suddenly a thought crept into my mind—what if it falls and explodes. I rushed out of the class only to find others doing the same. I closed my ears with my palms fearing a blast that would rip the building apart. It seems his cousin was a militant commander who had given the grenade to him for impressing his peers. A few days later, another student carried a pistol in the pocket of his trousers. He too had either borrowed it or had received it as a gift from a militant-relative. Expectedly, he too was mobbed by the classmates as everyone wanted to touch the pistol. Like a generous owner, he allowed each of us to hold it for a few seconds. Guns have always fascinated boys; I too was happy to have touched one.

Within days, a group of senior students marched to Fr Dominic's room and asked him to allow *namaz* in the school. Fr Dominic remained quiet and told them he would think about it. However, next day a few students organised *namaz* in the school compound during the recess. The school authorities ignored it and gradually, the attendance in *namaz* fell and eventually it was called off. In a few months, Fr Dominic and other Christian management staff of the school left for Jammu for good.

My world turned upside down.

In 1992, insurgency was at its peak when my father retired from the post of director in his department. As he had to give up the official house, our family shifted to our ancestral house in Ganderbal. Once again, I was happy to see the Sind flowing uninterrupted and to feel the soothing vibes coming from Qamar sahib's shrine. Life in Srinagar amidst militancy, violence, chaos, and slogan-shouting was a traumatic experience. It had left my mind scarred and my insides bruised. People like me and my friends had been raised with love and care and also a set of moral values. However, our daily encounter with violence, meeting people with crude countenances, the hate-mongers, others speaking of death and killings casually, made our lives miserable. In Srinagar, I was often depressed; at times I would cry quietly. I had realised that we were standing on shaky ground and living in uncertain times.

The early nineties was the most difficult time for a young person to live in Kashmir. Besides facing violence, Kashmir's social fabric was getting torn. Young men were getting sucked into the cycle of hate and violence; many crossed the Line of Control (LoC) from Kupwara-Uri side to Pakistan-occupied Kashmir (POK) where they got trained as militants in the camps. They returned with arms and the resolve to fight for *azadi* (independence). In the initial days, Jammu and Kashmir Liberation Front (JKLF) dominated the scene; people also called it Kashmir Liberation Front, probably in recognition of the fact that Jammu, the other part of the state, remained unimpressed with the idea of *azadi*.

Pakistan trained JKLF's cadres in arms handling and sabotage. However, they were only using JKLF—a known outfit—for a limited purpose and period. In hindsight it is clear that Pakistan used JKLF to trigger violence and to sow the idea of the *azadi* movement. The JKLF had once asked for an independent J&K, which meant that China, India, and Pakistan had to surrender the territory of undivided Jammu and Kashmir in their possession for this 'new nation'. Though its main ideologue Aman-ullah-Khan lived in Pakistan, he no longer enjoyed Islamabad's patronage. The Khan-headed JKLF was involved in skyjacking of an Indian Airlines plane to Lahore in 1971. Two young cousins from Kashmir, Hashim Qureshi, and Ashraf Qureshi had hijacked Srinagar-Amritsar flight and taken it to Lahore. The Fokker Friendship plane called *Ganga* was set ablaze by Pakistan after arresting the Qureshi brothers and release of all passengers. This act created animosity between India and Pakistan. Hashim has since returned to Kashmir with his family after serving a jail sentence in Pakistan and is now involved in peacemaking. Ashraf had settled in Pakistan where he died at the age of fifty-six.

However, JKLF's first leader in Kashmir was Mohammad Maqbool Bhat. He hailed from a small town of Trehgam in Kupwara. He was arrested for the murder of a bank manager and hanged in Delhi's Tihar jail for it in 1984. With the onset of militancy, JKLF cadres shot political leaders, Kashmiri Pandits who were active in social and political circles, media persons and some pro-India leaders. Its militants killed Judge Neelkanth Ganjoo, a Kashmiri Hindu who had convicted Maqbool Bhat of murder. Ganjoo was killed in the busy marketplace of Hari Singh High Street in Srinagar; his body lay there in a pool of blood for many hours.

However, soon the mandarins of insurgency in Pakistan—the ISI, army and the religious ideologues—realised that JKLF's complete independence idea was a threat to their country's existence. They also concluded that unless religion is injected into their plot on Kashmir, it would become increasingly difficult to get public support for the insurgency.

At this stage emerged the Hizbul Mujahideen, an outfit which believed in the merger of Kashmir with Pakistan and implementation of an Islamic jurisprudence—*Nizam-e-mustafa*—in Kashmir. Hizbul's rise led to a fratricidal war in Kashmir. Hizbul enjoyed Pakistan's full backing and, therefore, from the beginning had a clear edge in the turf war with JKLF. Gradually, JKLF's supplies of arms and cash from Pakistan dried up. Soon, the group lost some of its prominent ideologues like Dr Abdul Ahad Guru, a medical practitioner, and Professor Abdul Ahad Wani, Vice-chancellor of Kashmir University. Both were abducted by Hizbul militants and executed after being tortured.

Having lost control, the JKLF chief Yasin Malik donned a pacifist's garb; he invoked the name of Mahatma Gandhi and claimed his organisation had nothing to do with the gun. Looking back into history one can see that militancy in Kashmir had emerged out of clear thinking and planning on the part of Pakistani Generals, the ISI and the Army. Pakistan took full advantage of the anger and alienation of people triggered by the perceived rigging of elections by the then ruling National Conference in 1984. That year, some separatist leaders had cobbled a group, Muslim United Front (MUF) and contested the election under its banner. At the end of it, National Conference had emerged winner and the MUF and other opposition candidates blamed the government for rigging the results. One of the candidates who lost was Moulvi Mohammed Yousuf Shah, who later became the head of Hizbul Mujahideen and was given the fancy name of Syed Salahudeen. He left Kashmir to live in Islamabad-Rawalpindi. The JKLF cadres were drawn from a faction of National Conference who had called themselves Plebiscite Front. On the other hand, Hizbul Mujahideen militants were mostly drawn from Islamic Jamiat-ul-Tulba, the student wing of Jamat-e-Islami that had been secretly making inroads into colleges and institutions for decades.

Pakistan's plan was working—it had used JKLF to trigger chaos and insurgency and then dumped it for a more ideologically compatible Hizbul Mujahideen.

Ground Realities

I lived in Srinagar where birds no longer sang on their way to their nests built on branches and in crevices of trunks of old Chinar trees that dotted the city. Perhaps they did sing, but nobody heard them as their chatter was drowned in the crescendo of shrill slogans coming from neighbourhood mosques. Evenings in Srinagar were melancholic; with the approaching sunset, my stomach would churn in anticipation of the deafening night chorus. The sound blast from mosques violated the serenity of Jhelum that flowed close to my house. It was scary and disturbing; I couldn't focus on studies for my coming board examinations. The war cries of slogan-shouting brigades haunted me all night; rarely did I have a sound sleep those days.

It would all start soon after the muezzin called for prayers and the *namaz* was over. Going by the slogans they raised, it was clear that the agents of Pakistan were in control of mosques. These slogans left me more confused about the purpose of the ongoing armed rebellion. They would start with *Allahu Akbar* (Allah is greater), followed by the most irritating '*teri jaan meri jaan, Pakistan Pakistan*,' and '*Kashmir banega Pakistani*'. The final slogan would be '*hum kya chahte hain*: *azadi*, *azadi*'. This *tamasha* would end with a shoddy rendition of the *Quomi Tarana*, the national anthem of Pakistan—a Persian poem eulogising the land of the pure and Islamic symbols like the crescent.

My young mind failed to make sense of this. I often thought to myself that if the gunmen are genuinely fighting for *azadi* of Kashmir why are they supporting Pakistan? In a second scenario, if they are fighting against India and for Kashmir, why should they be asking Hindus to leave? How can someone stand for Pakistan and independence at the same time?

The environment in Srinagar was suffocating. Curfew, *hartal*, bomb blasts and death were what one had to wade through each day. My mother would be anxious while seeing the three of us—my brother, sister and me—off in the morning. I would invariably find her in the same state of anxiety and paranoia till we returned from school and college. Like most Kashmiri mothers, she would pray that none of her children be around when militants hurled a bomb in a marketplace or opened fire at the CRPF of a BSF bunker. The men in uniform hailing from different regions of India would retaliate and many times, civilians got killed and injured in the process. Thinking about it, I often felt depressed at home.

I was relieved to finish taking my board examination for class 12 in Srinagar. Soon, we packed all our belongings and moved to Ganderbal. My father had retired from service and it was only logical that we go back to our native place. In Srinagar, my father would often get upset at the daily disturbances and violence and blame New Delhi for not looking after the common Kashmiri. He would often crib that Delhi believed in keeping a handful of selfish leaders happy. "Delhi has alienated common people in Kashmir and only given monetary benefits to a select few," he would often say while reading the newspaper or discussing the situation with visitors.

INSIDE A MOSQUE

At Ganderbal, I realised that mosques had become epicenters of indoctrination and gun culture. I would always attend the Friday prayers in the local mosque, preferring to remain a low key devout standing in the last row of the assembly. At times, militants would join the congregation. The 'Commander' would often be led to the front row by members of his entourage. Mostly, a militant commander would be accompanied by four or five cadres, including his bodyguards. If the commander was a Pakistani, everyone in the assembly would be keen to see him. Though the militants wore same long flowing phirens, they could be identified by their kohl-rimmed eyes and long, flowing beards. Locals could make out a Pakistani among them through his body language, diction and looks; an outsider would be the cynosure of all eyes.

Inside mosques, militants flaunted their guns and before leaving hid them under their phirens. Most of the Pakistanis had 'bhai' suffixed to their code names. Bhai is a very north Indian expression, probably common among muhajirs in Pakistan. I failed to understand how it got linked to the insurgency; probably it was an acquired status symbol.

Before the *namaz*, the commander's bodyguard would meet the Imam and offer him Rs 500 to 1,500 as fees or donation in full public view. The tacit deal between the two was that the Imam would sing praises of the commander in his weekly sermon. It was a steady extra income for Imam Sahib. After the prayers, people would come to the front row to meet the commander and shake hands with him. Some elderly people even displayed their affection publicly and hugged him. People generally thought of militants as some kind of religious warriors. I too was fascinated by the Kalashnikov he would be holding. One day, I gathered courage to move to the front row and asked a militant accomplice of the commander if I could touch his gun. He smiled and permitted me to lift and hold it for a few seconds. I was excited and he could read my mind. He suddenly asked me, "Do you want one?"

"Yes."

"I can give you one, but for that you have to promise me that you will pray five times in the mosque," he said.

It didn't sound like a good bargain; I turned it down, politely. The militant also let it go but I could see the fading smile on his face.

One day in the summer of 1989, gun-wielding militants appeared at the Friday congregation at the mosque. One of them addressed the assembly and said there would be no annual fair at the Qamar sahib's shrine. Though nobody questioned him, the pindrop silence of the assembly was a loud hint of the general disapproval and shock. The speaker, however, was convinced that his diktat would be followed and he ignored the uneasy silence that followed his announcement. By now, Kashmiris had probably got used to such quirky diktats and nothing shocked them anymore. Displaying characteristic Kashmiri resilience they were ready to put up with any diktat to play safe. The speaker explained that holding celebrations and revering tombs were un-Islamic acts. Islam didn't permit worship of an icon, symbol or image and more so of a grave. Already, posters advising people not to celebrate the 'Urs' had appeared in the town.

The annual Urs at Qamar sahib's shrine is my best childhood memory. I had grown up with bright and joyous images of the two-day long annual festival at the shrine. Children used to wait eagerly for the day. That year, the shrine wore a deserted look; there was no cultural extravaganza on the banks of Sind. The river flowed quietly almost singing a muted sorrowful song as the believers in Qamar sahib's Sufi philosophy of 'love is God' and 'God is love' didn't visit him. I missed the sight of the tented and illuminated colony that popped up on the banks of the river overnight.

I missed the folk dancers and singers' performances that went on till late at night. During the festival, the riverfront looked like a *desi* Las Vegas. Children and elders tried their luck in makeshift casinos; smiling children swung their water balls in all directions; some could be seen enjoying joyrides and others coaxing their parents to part with money for buying a ticket for another ride.

I remember the hectic preparations at home for the Urs. Our family would get ready to receive guests from Srinagar. Many of our relatives and family friends would come in houseboats that glided on the Jhelum. My mother would engage a Waza—a Kashmiri chef—for preparing the multi-course lamb-rice feast for the guests. She also served food to the poor and the needy at the shrine. As children, on those two days we were permitted to be out till late night.

That year, the sight of the deserted shrine filled me with sadness and remorse. I could feel that entire Ganderbal was crying silently. I also felt guilty at not being able to prevent the dishonouring of Qamar sahib. However, the shrine continued to have visitors though only in a trickle. You could see the devout emerging out of the shrine in tears and saying silent prayers probably asking for forgiveness from their patron saint.

Qamar sahib was the soul of Ganderbal—invisible, without a form and shape—and yet so essential to the being of all humans. The gun-toting militants had attacked the soul of Ganderbal. Life in my favourite place on earth was never the same again. After a 25-year gap, even today the Urs remains the fondest memory of my childhood. I feel sad that the new generation has grown without feeling the spirit of Qamar sahib.

I took admission in Sri Pratap College in Srinagar. Every morning, I would take a public transport bus to Srinagar. Quite often, I would have armed militants as my co-passengers. Each time a bearded young man with a gun boarded the bus, a hushed silence fell inside. I noticed that the militants would stare at women passengers who would squirm in their seats and try to make a huddle as if drawing strength from each other's presence against a predator. Everyone noticed this and yet chose to ignore it.

Sometimes, if a posse of CRPF or BSF men intercepted our bus for security check, we would freeze. The presence of militants and a possible confrontation between them and security forces was a good possibility. The very thought of it sent a chill down our spines. As the bus came to a halt on the orders of force personnel, the militant would quickly dump his gun in the lap of a woman passenger, who, in turn would hide it under her long flowing dupatta or burqa. The forces didn't search the women even as they could see their faces turning pale and some of them shivering in fear.

Gradually, I realised that the gun was being used to settle personal scores and secure individual interests and not for an ideology or a political cause. It had led to a class war in Kashmir, even though the outside world believed it was a manifestation of peoples' yearning for *azadi*.

The inherent rivalries of JKLF and Hizbul mujahideen had divided the Kashmiri society and the movement too. In my neighbourhood, boys joined either group depending on their family's background. I belonged to the Sheikh clan and had I wanted to pick up the gun, I would have to opt for the JKLF. On the other hand, for the Sofi boys—mostly from the families of artisans, landless agriculturists, tillers and small traders—Hizbul mujahideen was a natural choice.

The gang wars between the two groups were common. They would target each other's families to avenge old grudges and injustices. The Sheikhs were seen as a clan with large swathes of land and part of the ruling elite—favoured in jobs, getting into professional colleges and other nominated positions in the government.

With each passing day, the rivalries between JKLF and Hizbul were growing and causing more bloodletting. After all, Pakistan had lost three wars with India and it nursed a deep resentment against Kashmiris for not helping its non-state actors—tribesmen from NWFP who raided Kashmir twice. Now they seemed to have devised a great plan: use Kashmiris against India. This way the blood of Kashmiris and Indians would flow while Pakistan's losses would be minimal. My extended family was also targeted; the houses of some of my uncles were burnt and their young boys had to remain in hiding for days to escape being killed by the Hizbul. Eventually, a couple of cousins had to join JKLF for saving the lives of their family members.

However, the fights would be more intense and long drawn if rival militants had fallen in love with the same woman. No doubt, women played the role of informers for the militants; they would pass on the buzz about the neighbourhood to them based on which they would select their targets for killing, abduction and extortion. For this reason, militants mostly stayed with the economically weaker families and often befriended their women and paid cash too. The militants were trigger happy and flaunted their power, especially to attract women.

I could write an epic if everyone in Kashmir spoke honestly about the humiliation and harassment suffered by them at the hands of militants those years.

Besides JKLF and Hizb, small groups comprising petty criminals had emerged in many towns. They had somehow got hold of the easily available guns but were neither trained in their proper use nor did they have the courage to take on the security forces. The gun helped them in extorting money from the common people and lure girls. These gunmen were trigger happy and hardly knew how to fight the forces. People appeased them too since nobody wanted to take a chance.

One day, while returning from college, I noticed the commotion in our *mohalla*. I was told that a particular 'commander-in-chief' of a *tanzeem* (militant group) had announced he would launch an attack on the CRPF convoy and ordered people to remain indoors. Some people in the lane were rushing to the nearest safe place; women were frantically looking for their children who could be playing in the neighbourhood ; some hysterically called for their sons and daughters. The 'commander' had positioned himself on the top floor of a house with a gun slung over his shoulder. I heard gunshots. It didn't look like there was retaliation but I feared that the CRPF men would soon enter our area in search of the attackers.

Later, we came to know that an eighty-year-old neighbour who was sitting in the window of his house was killed in the firing. The CRPF was nowhere around; their convoy had passed on the Kangan-Srinagar road located three km away from the point where the 'commander' was stationed. However, next day the newspapers carried a report that an eighty-year-old Kashmiri was killed by the CRPF. The people of Ganderbal knew the truth and were shocked at the media's failure to project it.

Truth was dying every moment in Kashmir and we could do nothing about it.

The fact is that militants of both JKLF and Hizbul Mujahideen often used barbaric means to kill, abduct and torture their victims. The monthly 'fees' the militants levied from contractors, businessmen and employees ran into crores of rupees. They didn't even spare foreign tourists, many of whom were abducted and later released for a ransom that was paid quietly, often by the governments of their countries.

Women were most unsafe in Kashmir. Some 'commanders' forced rich and influential people to marry their daughters to them. I remember once a highly placed bureaucrat who was my father's close friend came to our house. He cried on my father's shoulders. It seems an illiterate local militant commander had asked for the hand of his daughter in marriage. A 'yes' would be unthinkable and a 'no' could even cost him his life. Finally, he had to marry off his daughter to the 'commander'. She was widowed after a few years as her militant husband was killed in a counter-insurgency operation. Another friend of my father had to marry his daughter to his driver's son, who was a commander. He did it with humiliation and with a heavy heart.

MISSING PANDITS

Many of my father's pandit friends had left Kashmir after they were given a Hobson's choice—leave or get ready to die. Some good-hearted Muslim neighbours had also advised them to play safe by leaving. They too believed that Hindus could return in a few months since the situation would become normal by then.

My father's friends like Krishenji of Karan Nagar, Zaroo uncle of Jawahar Nagar, advocate Tikoo were packing their bags when he came to know it. He called each one and tried to dissuade them from leaving. Soon, his close friend Lassa Koul, Director, Doordarshan, Srinagar, was killed in cold blood in

Srinagar. Koul, a handsome man lived inside a high security zone close to his office and never ventured out without a retinue of security cars and gunmen. One day, he felt so homesick for his old parents that he went to see them without confiding in his security men. As he was nearing his house, the gunmen belonging to JKLF opened fire killing him on the spot.

I remember, after Koul's assassination, my father's face was wreathed in sorrow and pain. I also remember his profound soliloquy: Pakistan has made deep inroads into the Kashmiri society; it has managed to poison the Kashmiri youth through a sustained propaganda for four years.

Even as we saw Hindus were leaving Kashmir in hordes, nobody thought they had left for good; everyone believed they would return after winter as possibly by then the situation in Kashmir would be normal. That year, many Hindus and Muslim Kashmiri neighbours met in Jammu—in the middle of its sun-soaked roads, restaurants and especially meat shops. Everyone hoped the situation in Kashmir would be fine soon for them to return. No Kashmiri was prepared to live in the arid heat of the north Indian summer.

However, nearly three decades later, they are yet to return home.

My father would often advise his Hindu friends against selling their land, houses, and other immovable assets in the Valley. He was also against some greedy Muslim buying their properties at throwaway prices. He was so perturbed that he sent a petition to the government seeking its intervention in checking the desperate sale of Hindu houses, land and other properties. He had asked the government to declare all sales involving properties of Hindus till 2000 null and void. Ultimately he had to give up his campaign after his Hindu friends told him that they needed to sell their property to support the education of their children.

Beards And Ideology

In the beginning, everyone thought the unrest and the armed rebellion in Kashmir were all about *azadi*—the movement for freedom. People across the Valley, especially in towns and the capital Srinagar were brimming with enthusiasm and anxiety thinking of the incoming dramatic turn of events. People generally didn't dislike the idea of *azadi* even though nobody had clarity on what we wanted to be free of. In short, there was no identified enemy. Even in my family, the *azadi* sentiment was not perceived as a threat to our beliefs which were: we are Indians and Kashmir is an inalienable part of India. Nobody had ever imagined that Kashmir would soon get drenched in blood and the Valley turned into a theatre of gore.

The pioneers of the *azadi* movement were four young men whose group was popularly known as the HAJY group. HAJY was an acronym for (Abdul) Hameed Sheikh, Ashfaq

Majid Wani, Javed Sheikh *'Nalka'* and Yasin Malik. All of them were members of a radical group—Islamic Students League (ISL), an underground organisation opposed to India. They were the new age heroes of Kashmir. In fact, ISL had shot into prominence during the first international cricket test match played between India and West Indies in Srinagar. The emergence of ISL is unwittingly described by journalist-blogger Abhishek Mukherjee, who was covering the match back then. He writes: As soon as the two teams had entered the Chinar-fringed Sher-e-Kashmir stadium on the morning of October 13, 1983, a section of the spectators had started heckling the Indians. The hooting and commotion went on all through the play and in-between one could even hear a stray pro-Pakistan slogan. In the break time, a few boys also entered the playfield and tried to damage the wicket.

That was the first and last international cricket match played in Kashmir.

The ISL members were rounded up but nobody took their presence as a serious threat to peace. The police treated them as miscreants hired by the Pro-Pakistan fringe that had always tried to cause embarrassment to the governments in Srinagar and Delhi. This residual group of pro-Pakistanis was treated with utter disdain by people and, therefore, they had always maintained a low profile.

The hanging of JKLF leader Maqbool Bhat in Tihar jail on February 11, 1984, helped the ISL rise from the ashes. Bhat was a Kashmiri hailing from Trehgam village in north Kashmir. He was the co-founder of the Jammu and Kashmir National Liberation Front (JKNLF) with Amanullah Khan. Khan hailed from Gilgit in the Pakistan occupied territory and didn't speak Kashmiri. Bhat was first arrested for killing an intelligence officer in the border district of Kupwara in 1966. The court awarded him death and he was lodged in Srinagar jail. Two years later, Bhat escaped through a tunnel that he had painstakingly bored from inside his prison cell and fled to Pakistan. Once again he became an active campaigner for independent Jammu and Kashmir. Bhat returned to Kashmir in 1974. This time, he was on a mission to recruit local youth for a 'liberation' campaign. His mission was nipped in the bud as he was arrested in Langet, a small village close to the Line of Control, as he was fleeing once again towards POK, after looting a bank and killing its manager. This time, the authorities took no chances with Bhat's security; he was lodged in Delhi's high-security Tihar jail.

In the meanwhile, in UK, Amanullah Khan and his associates hatched a plan to get Bhat released. In February 1984, the JKNLF men abducted Indian diplomat Ravinder Mhatre in Birmingham. He was abducted as he was alighting from a bus. In fact, it was his daughter Asha's birthday and he was carrying a cake. His abductors had planned to hold him as a captive to get Bhat released. However, at some stage, the plan floundered and they killed the 47-year-old Mhatre. All the abductors and their mentor Khan fled to Pakistan. Scotland Yard had lost too much time in understanding the plot and acted late. The UK cops could arrest only two persons who were later convicted for Mhatre's murder.

Mhatre's murder shook Delhi and suddenly attention shifted to Bhat. Files moved quickly for the President who, as per the script, rejected his mercy petition that lay on his table for seven years. Bhat was hanged in Tihar jail on February 11, 1984, and buried in its graveyard. His supporters saw his hanging as Indian state's revenge for Mahatre. It rejuvenated the *azadi* brigade and gave a fresh cause to groups like ISL in Kashmir to raise peoples' passions.

In 1987, a motley group of anti-India outfits decided to contest elections under the banner of Muslim United Front (MUF). The coming together of these groups led to a lot of speculations and buzz. Some believed these groups had got tired of fighting and wanted to join mainstream politics while others looked at this development with suspicion. As a young activist, Yasin Malik volunteered for the election management team of Syed Mohammad Yusuf Shah, the MUF candidate from the Amira Kadal Assembly constituency in Srinagar. As the counting of votes was underway and the chances of Shah's win looked bright, it is said that on the instructions of Chief Minister Farooq Abdullah, the presiding officer rather surreptiously declared the candidate of the ruling National Conference a winner. The public perception is that Abdullah had apparently used the state machinery to subvert the results. He probably felt unnerved at the emergence of another political force and a potential challenger to his party's hegemony. Malik and others were rounded up and given a thrashing inside a police station. Shah, a former cleric, now lives in Rawalpindi with a new identity—he is chief of the Hizbul Mujahideen and has acquired a new name of Syed Salahudeen. A cleric (maulvi) hailing from a small central Kashmir village of Soibugh, Salahudeen has also become the first Kashmiri to be declared a global terrorist by the USA!

The young Malik's mind was seething with anger and revenge.

Malik and other members of the HAJY group were to soon cross the unguarded LOC from Kupwara in north Kashmir to reach POK where they received a rousing welcome from Pakistan's spy agency, the Inter-Services Intelligence, ISI. They were trained in firing guns, throwing grenades on targets and a couple of months later, sent back with arms, ammunition, and a roadmap for creating chaos in Kashmir. Kashmir was agog with rumours that youth were going to Pakistan for 'training' by simply boarding public transport buses at Srinagar's Batmaloo bus stand. Conductors of buses would shout *"Kaupwor, appor"* (Kupwara and across) to lure all the potential militants. The buzz was that huge consignments of guns and grenades had reached Kashmir. People scarcely believed these reports and many took it as hearsay and propaganda.

A few grenades had exploded here and there in Srinagar, yet no major causalities happened. However, the HAJY group got exposed with its involvement in the abduction of a young medico Rubaiya Saeed while she was travelling in a public transport bus in Srinagar. Rubaiya was the daughter of the then Home Minister of India, Mufti Mohammad Saeed. Her captors wanted to get five militants—Sheikh Abdul Hameed, Ghulam Nabi Butt, Noor Mohammad Kalwal, Mohammad Altaf and Mushtaq Zarger—released from jail in lieu of her; they won this round.

As soon as the five were released and Dr Rubaiya reached home spontaneous celebrations were seen in Srinagar. People poured out on the streets to show their support for the JKLF and the released militants. Women sang traditional songs and danced to welcome them as if they were warriors returning home after a victory.

A year later, Ashfaq Wani died in an encounter with BSF in Srinagar downtown; three years later, Hamid Sheikh got drowned in the Jhelum while trying to escape from the security forces in the same area. Yasin Malik was arrested and later released. He renounced the gun and violence and married a Pakistani woman. Javed Nalka remains a low key separatist till today.

Ever since Hizbul Mujahideen (HM) was emerging on the scene, JKLF was losing its popularity and support. Hizbul emerged from rural areas and its militants were more ruthless than the apparently Rambo-type JKLF's urban leaders. Hizbul's open talk of the struggle being about Islam's supremacy and support for Pakistan made many Kashmiris rethink about their support to the 'movement'. Suddenly, the romantic notion of *azadi* had vanished and the reality of violence being an intrinsic part of the 'movement' hit everyone. This eventually led to cracks in Kashmiri people's once unflinching support for *azadi*.

The euphoria of *azadi* was over.

In Ganderbal, HM's coming was announced through posters. One fine morning, townsfolk woke up to find posters announcing that the struggle in Kashmir was for *Nizam-e-Mustafa* (The rule of Allah) and *jihad* was the only way to get it. The posters clearly hinted that it was a religious war. The subsequent incidents were soon to trigger a class war in Kashmiri society. The ground rule was the underdogs like the scions of *Jamait-e-Islami* and hardcore Islamists families would join the HM while the 'haves' of the society—families like ours—would be part of the JKLF.

Their rivalries subsumed everyone and it was getting difficult for people to remain neutral.

The ideological rivalry between HM and JKLF had entered the schools and colleges. As I saw the growing visibility and influence of Hizbul supporters around me, I was reminded of how militants had banned the Urs at Qamar Sahib's shrine and how the campaign was started through posters that had been put up on all walls and spaces in my town. I was fast realising that the real targets of militants were not only a handful of non-Muslims but the majority of Kashmiri Muslims, who believed in the Sufi school of Islam.

Kashmiris practised the Islam of Sufis. The practice of Islam was more about syncretism—without compromising on the fundamentals of religion. A miniscule group of religious extremists had always been against this culture. The same group had now re-emerged as powerful entities like Hizbul Mujahideen and a resurgent Jamait-e-Islami, whose cadres were advisors and overground supporters of the former. For them, offering prayers at the mausoleums was akin to idol worship—they called it *kufr*. This development only re-affirmed my belief that Kashmiris cannot protect their religious beliefs by becoming part of Pakistan; we are safe in multi-religious and secular country like India. With the help of the gun, the extremists were enforcing their brand of Saudi Arab-type Islam on the people.

In the early nineties, many political leaders had fled Kashmir; the administration had either collapsed or was in limbo. Across Kashmir militants ruled the roost. It was a war unleashed by Pakistan through their stooges on the common man of Kashmir. This kind of war has no rules, morals or ethical values.

The JKLF's claim that its members had picked up the gun for restoring the dignity and freedom of Kashmir and Hizbul Mujahideen's promise to turn the Valley into an ideal Islamic state were all hogwash. Both groups indulged in barbaric killings and torture and some members extorted money to release their captives. The contractors, businessmen and employees etc. were made to pay the 'movement fund' regularly. Even foreign tourists were not spared; many were abducted and some let off for ransom; others were not so lucky and have remained untraced till today.

It was becoming clear to me that Pakistan was taking revenge on the people of Kashmir for belying its expectations of an instantaneous uprising when it had sent tribesmen to liberate the Valley in 1948. Islamabad had repeatedly failed to trigger rebellion in Kashmir; it had waged three wars with India and lost all. Instead of annexing Kashmir, Islamabad had lost its eastern flank. Therefore, this time, Pakistan had embarked on a plan to kill many birds with one stone; the people of Kashmir were major sufferers in this.

THE CAMPUS LIFE

In my college, I could see the trend of flowing beards among youth catching up fast. Their faces were wreathed in rage. Many of our college boys carried pistols and grenades and displayed them to intimidate others.

With each passing day, the gang of bearded students was feeling emboldened. In Srinagar's Shri Pratap College, they would intimidate and bully others. A bearded student could waylay anyone inside the campus and ask him why he didn't have a beard; he could question his faith and ask him whether he supported the movement. One day, a bearded fellow asked me why I had a sticker with 'Rebel' written on it pasted on my scooter. He asked me if I was trying to cobble a new group of liberals in the college and was that the reason why I had pasted this sticker on my vehicle. I got angry and didn't even make an effort to hide my feelings. I physically restrained him from touching my scooter. I told him I would remove the sticker myself. This led to a scuffle and he hit me on my face.

The infighting between bearded boys and others was becoming a common practice. Often some of the bearded boys would carry pistols and unarmed people like me would discreetly avoid getting into a confrontation or an argument with them. This, however, was only helping them as they would rag, bully and physically attack others.

This trend got me worried. I thought I had to fight them for my survival. Four months later, I had founded Jammu and Kashmir Students United Forum (JKSUF) with just ten members. Our mission was to oppose the ideas of the 'bearded gang' and check its forays into campus politics. When we announced the formation of our front, the bearded guys were livid with anger. A real war of wits started. It was an open clash of ideas and ideology; one side had guns while the other was full of ideas and arguments. However, at times, we also managed to show off an odd firearm that one could easily obtain from the local militant commander. This helped strike a balance of power in the campus.

Back then Srinagar was full of self-styled commanders and *tanzeems* (militant organisations). Many were running protection services for those feeling threatened and vulnerable. Our union would also buy such support on occasions against our rivals. We would seek strategic alliances with small militant groups that were also opposed to the domination of Hizbul Mujahideen. This way, we had managed to curtail the powers of the bearded gang; they were no longer omnipotent.

Life on the campus was not easy; we had to be on guard against troublemakers and take a great deal of care to confine our differences with rivals to ideologies and not provoke them into using guns. However, since the other side was pro-active, at times, we would get into serious trouble. One day, a member of our group was killed in a shootout in the college. Another day bearded guys swooped on my office in Dal Gate and ransacked it.

The killing and vandalism did subdue me and others; my desperation was growing.

One day, a gentleman entered my office in the college. He didn't look like a Kashmiri. Without wasting time, he said he was a friend and appreciated the work of our organization. I am yet to know his real identity.

However, at this stage the world seemed to be greatly interested in Kashmir. Those days, ambassadors and other foreign leaders would visit Kashmir regularly to have a first-hand understanding of the situation. They would visit Badami Bagh Cantonment, Hurriyat office, and homes of separatist leaders and also meet members of the civil society. Our group always met the visiting leaders and presented before them the case of how terrorism had spoilt Kashmir's ethos.

I would be invariably allowed to meet them as leader of the youth group. Most of the diplomats would intently listen to my ideas. I told them the realities that often a politician would never want them to know. So when my colleagues and I would tell them the real stories of people under the militant's gun and how they were caught between security forces and terrorists, most of them took copious notes. I remember my meeting with Susan Grace, the first secretary of the Australian High Commission, in Hotel Grand Palace. I also met envoys of UK, Finland and European Union. Many embassies would call me to Delhi for discussions and for drawing up a possible roadmap for resolution of Kashmir.

Many diplomats would ask me a simple question, "What are your future plans?" Like most people of my age, I had no idea of the future.

"I really haven't thought about it," I would say.

Many of them advised me to continue creating awareness among the youth in Kashmir. Since they didn't have a direct stake in Kashmir and hence no vested interest, I valued their opinion. It was encouraging. Suddenly, I felt confident and cared for; I was no longer lonely and isolated. In the coming days, we created a wing of JKSUF in the Kashmir University and formed a core group of fifteen girls and ten boys.

I must admit the women were more focused on fighting terrorism in their own way. I am restraining myself from giving credit to many women who have silently played a key role in exposing terrorists. A number of militant commanders, especially foreign mercenaries, made contact with local women and had girlfriends. At times, these were school or college-going students. The militants would have long conversations with them on mobile phones. As it happens at that age, the 'girlfriends' would share the conversation with their close friends. As such, the 'girlfriends' enjoyed an exalted status among their peers for their proximity to the 'mujahid'.

The mobile conversations and the leaked details of their conversations have given away locations of many a dreaded terrorist to the security forces.

The JKSUF organised seminars and published literature about issues confronting the youth and the society at large. Interestingly, our members would also join stone pelting mobs in streets to create a smokescreen about our mission. There was no point is showing bravado; it was better to be seen as part of a big crowd for us to continue our work. This is the harsh reality of Kashmir even today.

To give just one instance of how ordinary Kashmiris helped crack the inner circles of terrorists and their over ground networks, I remember a friend who had managed to get precise details about a top Kashmiri businessman, who was running a hawala racket for terror groups. My friend had somehow managed to get close to the businessman's nephew. Gradually, the debonair nephew admitted that his uncle was so influential that each day he would receive one crore rupees in his account and he would withdraw the money the same afternoon. The money or part of it was meant for financing activities of terrorists and sustaining the lifestyle of separatist leaders. This led to unearthing and dismantling of the biggest network of terror financing in Kashmir.

Honestly, my teammates and I feel proud to have played a small role in generating hope and optimism and not bowing to the diktats of terrorists and troublemakers.

Those days an incident happened that changed the course of my life. One day, I was accompanied by a teammate and his girlfriend while we were walking in Srinagar. Suddenly, some youth started teasing the woman accompanying us; this infuriated us and we got into a heated argument with them. Soon it snowballed into a scuffle. One of them was a small-time political activist and a rich guy and he started chasing us in his car. My friend and I were shocked by his audacity. We somehow managed to stop him and snatch the keys of his car.

Soon, we found the police had reached the spot. Apparently he had called the police. Since we were in a tearing hurry, I spoke rudely to the policeman. He bundled the two of us—the woman was asked to go home—in his van and eventually in the lockup. When my parents came to get me out on bail, I remember the police officer telling them that I was involved in criminal activities. My parents stood with me. My father told him that he had full faith in his son and also that the law would take its own course. The Court acquitted me in due course.

That episode changed my outlook on life. While I was inside the lockup, a local terrorist of the Lashkar-e-Taiba was also there. He was treated like a King—the policemen served him chicken, carried a pail of hot water for him to bathe and offered him cigarettes. He was arrested by the Special Operations Group (SOG), the anti-terror squad of the Police.

That lockup experience had changed something inside me. I realised that we have to work for strengthening institutions so that the terrorists would not be feted inside the police stations. I was even more determined to take my fight to a bigger stage and logical conclusion.

At The United Nations

I had finished my college and was in no hurry to tread the conventional career path. In fact, I was quite happy being a political activist; little did I know that my life was going to change soon. In the spring of 1999, I received a letter from the United Nations Commission for Human Rights (UNCHR), Geneva, for attending its 55th session. I was invited as a representative of the Delhi-based NGO Himalayan Research and Cultural Foundation set up by a renowned Kashmiri academician Prof K Warikoo.

The very thought of representing India at the UN was exhilarating. After all, at twenty-three, not many would get this privilege. I was nervous and had no idea how I should prepare for the event. My identity as an Indian-Kashmiri was my greatest strength; I had lived through the Valley's turmoil and tried to make a difference to the situation. I was no VIP but a common man in the street who tried to resist the creed of terrorism and its ideology imposed by outsiders. My faith in my spiritual guide Qamar Sahib and my country was unshakeable.

Amidst this, I had to face a comic situation at home. When I told my mother I was going to Geneva to speak at the UN, she laughed. "I know, you must be going to Delhi or Banglore," she said. Even my siblings reacted likewise. So, when I left for Geneva nobody knew where I was headed.

In Delhi, I met Dr Riyaz Punjabi, a renowned Kashmiri academician, who later became the vice-chancellor of the University of Kashmir. After getting my visa from the Swiss embassy without hassle, I went to see him in his office in South Delhi from where he published a peace journal. Like hundreds of intellectuals, Punjabi had to leave Kashmir after terrorists killed Kashmir University's Vice-Chancellor, Prof Mushirul Hassan and his secretary Abdul Ghani Zargar in 1990.

Punjabi was a warm person. He helped me book the hotel in Geneva and put my anxieties to rest. He also gave me some quick tips on travelling alone. I was relieved to know that we would stay in the same hotel in Geneva. Prof Wariko had already left for Geneva and Punjabi and I were taking different flights on the same day.

At the Indira Gandhi International Airport's immigration counter, I presented my passport and ticket to the officer on duty. "What is the purpose of your visit?" he asked me in a gruff and somewhat intimidating voice. I told him that I was going to speak at the UN conference. After a meaningful silence, he asked me to come inside a cubicle. I knew I was being detained. Those days anyone would view a young Kashmiri Muslim travelling to the UN with suspicion; they thought what if he spoke against India? Does he have permission from the authorities? Dr Punjabi's tips came in handy and I remained calm during the two-and-a-half-hours of detention. After initial questioning, the officer went out and perhaps spoke to his seniors. My flight would take off in fifteen minutes and here I was waiting for permission to board it. I was worried and getting restless. I didn't want to miss the chance. Finally, when the officer gave me the go ahead and asked me to rush, I realised I was the last passenger to board the Austrian Airlines flight to Geneva via Vienna.

The plane landed at Geneva airport at about 7.30 am. As I came out, cool air caressed my face. I was looking at the bluest skies and the most enchanting scenery all around. I took several deep breaths, tying to inhale the divine and fragrant ambience. On the way to my hotel located at Lake Geneva, I thought about Kashmir. Since my birth, I was made to believe that Kashmir is the most beautiful place on earth and, therefore, a paradise. There was no doubt in my mind that the world envied us for the scenic splendour of our land.

That day, what lay around me was enough to shatter my childhood belief. The real paradise on earth was here, in front of me—Geneva. The city is traversed by lakes with a breathtaking backdrop of snow-capped peaks. In short, Geneva offers everything that Kashmir has in terms of natural beauty with a small yet significant difference. Here, every space looks so spic and span; even the air is fragrant and public spaces inviting. I was telling myself that while Nature can shower its bounties on a land, to preserve and value that God's gift is up to the people who live on the land. Keeping a city clean is a culture and an ethos. In Kashmir we tend to always pass on this responsibility to the government. As a Kashmiri, I could make out that we had been using our lakes and cities for dumping urban trash, and during the years of insurgency, the powerful people had wantonly destroyed jungles, usurped public land and even managed to create artificial gardens and islands inside the Dal Lake for commercial use.

From the window of my room in Hotel Drake, I could see the splendidly calm Geneva Lake with crystal clear water and I took a deep breath, closed my eyes and almost lapsed into a meditative mood. Suddenly, I saw my soul leave my body; it was gliding over the hills and valleys of Kashmir. My body lay listless and was being buried in Kashmir. As I opened my eyes, I literally felt my soul had travelled to Heaven. My mind was lighter; a burden that most of us carry in Kashmiri was off my head. This was a born-again spiritual experience.

I suddenly felt liberated.

After relaxing for an hour or so in the hotel, I left for the UN office with Dr Punjabi. It was a grandiose building with flags of all the member countries fluttering outside. To me, the only familiar landmark was the adjoining building of the International Committee of Red Cross (ICRC). I had seen ICRC vans moving on Srinagar roads; its officials would visit jails and detention centers to check the living conditions of the inmates there. Their presence added to Kashmir's credentials as a conflict zone.

As Dr Punjabi was a veteran UN speaker, he was quite influential in the building; almost everyone knew him and people greeted him with warmth. I was lucky to be guided by him in everything—right from picking up my identity papers to finalising my speech. After getting the mandatory papers, we settled down for a brief chat in the lobby. Like a kind teacher, he told me that the purpose of our visit was to counter Pakistan's propaganda on Kashmir. This should be the focus of our official speeches at the session and also in our interactions with other delegates and diplomats. Islamabad's strategy was to malign India for committing atrocities in Kashmir. In its narrow worldview, the Pakistanis projected Kashmir as a case of a 'Hindu' army trying to crush a 'Muslim' rebellion in Kashmir.

Dr Punjabi took me around the UN lobby and introduced me to many activists and diplomats. Most were happy and some even surprised to see a young Kashmiri Muslim coming from Srinagar. Next day, I met Mary Robinson, chairperson of the UNHRC in the lobby. She told me that everybody was waiting to listen to my speech at the session. I suddenly realised the huge importance of my work there.

Two days later, I was supposed to make a formal speech at the session.

It seems my presence had created a flutter in the Pakistani camp. While moving in the lobby, Dr Punjabi had pointed towards the Pakistani delegation—its members were in a huddle in one corner of the huge hall. He had cautioned me enough about their machinations. Later, I came to know that the Pakistanis believed I was a non-Kashmiri. They had called up the Hurriyat Conference leaders in Kashmir to know more about my antecedents. I could see Pakistanis whispering to each other and brazenly staring at me. It was embarrassing.

However, I ignored them and moved around meeting people from different parts of the world.

Pakistan presented an imaginary narrative at the UN. It was: Indian forces are killing Muslims in Kashmir. Their speakers often flaunted clippings of Indian newspapers as proof of the 'atrocities'. All pictures of slain terrorists and civilians who may have died in crossfire between terrorists and security forces and persons killed by terrorists were all shown as victims of Indian 'atrocities'.

Both the countries did a lot of canvassing in the UN lobby.

Punjabi and Warikoo were regulars at the UN meet; occasionally, other Kashmiris like advocate Ashok Bhan and journalist Asrar Sultanpuri also joined them. All of them had personally suffered at the hands of terrorists and had to leave Kashmir for safety. Pakistanis would try to provoke them by pointing out they were not living in Kashmir and, therefore, their version of the situation was not authentic.

Had I not come to Geneva, I would have never realised that Kashmir was a multi-dimensional warfare. Apart from combating terrorism on the ground, we had to expose Pakistan's gameplan in Kashmir before the world. At the UN, I was pitted against terrorists masquerading as human rights defenders on the Pakistan side. Honestly, I never felt as angry at Pakistan as I did when I saw a former JKLF terrorist in his new *avatar* as a peacenik.

Kashmir, in fact, was a big talking point in the lobby of the UN.

On the first day, I was jetlagged and desperately wanted to rest and therefore asked Punjabi for permission to call it a day. He asked me to buy mutton on my way to the hotel as he had decided to cook dinner. Following his directions, I reached a meat shop downtown. Salman, the shopkeeper, introduced himself as a Pakistani. He was quite excited to see me, another fellow South Asian. However, he took me for an Afghan. When I told him I was from Kashmir, he kept staring at me for a good one minute. He wanted to know from me about the situation in Kashmir. Salman told me that he felt terribly sad for Kashmiri people as they faced brutalities of the Indian Army. It seemed he and his friends wanted to donate money to save the Muslims of Kashmir, on Eid.

Interrupting Salman's breathless soliloquy, I assured him that I would return in two days and we would discuss Kashmir. When I went to see Salman again he was waiting with two of his compatriots. They seemed to be genuinely inquisitive about Kashmir and were not the argumentative types.

I told them that Kashmiri Muslims were facing violence unleashed by terrorists sent by Pakistan. I also explained to them that in Kashmir Islam was flourishing and not in danger; India is a secular nation and its army comprises men of all religions and not only Hindus. I told them the J&K police, which has many Muslims, was fighting terrorists and its personnel were laying down their lives in the fight.

As I spoke, a hushed silence fell in the shop. Sensing that my message was well received, I told them I was afraid the donations they paid for Kashmir must have gone into funding the lifestyles of Kashmir's separatist leaders. At this they looked meaningfully at each other. Another spell of silence fell on them and it took Salman a while to break it. He also spoke in a low and almost conspiratorial tone. He said of late he and his friends had become wary of the motives of Kashmiri fund collectors. The reason was that some of the fund-collectors had acquired big properties in Switzerland and other parts of Europe. After knowing this, Salman suspected the properties must have been bought with funds collected for Kashmir.

I also struck an instant friendship with Showkat Kashmiri, a well known human rights campaigner from Pakistan occupied Kashmir now living as a refugee in Geneva. Showkat had raised his voice against repression of political activists by the Pakistani Army in his part of Kashmir. His party espoused the cause of *azadi* from Pakistan. Hours before the ISI had sent assassins for him, Showkat had managed to flee the country and take shelter in Geneva.

He told me about his life in Muzaffarabad, capital of POK. It seems most residents of Muzaffarabad and other towns of POK live in the Gulf and other countries as there are no jobs back home. Unlike in Kashmir, Pakistan had not developed areas under its control, so the majority of the people were forced to seek work abroad. We also had conversations about conditions in our respective chunks of Kashmir. I realised that the key difference between the two was the system of education. While in Jammu and Kashmir, we have plenty of educational institutions, POK had no major institutions. Showkat told me that Pakistan military was corrupt and the Generals had parked their wealth outside the country; many owned mansions in London and Riyadh. From his account I could understand that Pakistan was treating people of POK shabbily. I felt blessed to have been born in Indian-Kashmir where the system had given me full rights and stakes in deciding my future.

The Pakistani delegation at the UN comprised mostly Punjabis and had just one Kashmiri speaker.

In the UN lobby, I met an American, Usman Rahim. In his casual attire and overgrown hair, he almost looked like a hippie. His American accent and oodles of flamboyance set him apart from the serious looking people around. I often saw him in the company of the UK-based Barrister Abdul Ahad Tramboo. He introduced himself as a JKLF activist and claimed his great-grandfather had lived in Kashmir. That sounded interesting. When I prodded him for his Kashmir links, Usman had no idea about the place of his family origins in Kashmir. There was something that I didn't like about him; he was always playing to the galleries and seeking attention. He had an NGO that worked on environment. One day, he told me he was quite upset with the Indian army for its role in destroying Kashmir's forests. I was livid at his brazen remarks and asked him curtly if he ever cared about Pakistan Army's track record on the environment.

One day Usman told me that he had links with American intelligence agencies. I couldn't figure out if he was trying to project an image of an influential person or telling the truth. Somehow, I could never trust him.

Years later, in the summer of 2004, Usman Rahim appeared in Srinagar as head of *Mercy Crops*, an environmental NGO. He had opened a well-equipped office close to the house of separatist leader Mirwaiz Moulvi Umer Farooq at Naseem Bagh. A number of local youth got jobs at his office and he paid them good salaries. In no time Usman became a regular visitor to Chief Minister Omar Abdullah's office. *Mercy Crops* organised seminars and conferences where separatist leaders and senior officials of the government were invited. New Delhi knew Usman's links with Pakistan yet it took three years to deport him. I was always wary of his intentions and felt he must have set up his shop in Kashmir to facilitate financing of separatists. Interestingly, Shehla Rashid, who later emerged as a left-wing student leader of the Jawahar Lal Nehru University (JNU), New Delhi, was working as coordinator of *Mercy Crops*.

In Geneva, I also made friends with Mehraj Baloch, a Pakistani from the restive region of Balochistan, who was living as a refugee in Geneva. He told me stories about Pakistan army's atrocities. Baloch people were a nation till 1947. Soon after its formation, Pakistan usurped the land of the fiercely independent people through subterfuge. Baloch nationalists were asking for freedom from Pakistan and in response the army had let loose a reign of repression. Members of the nationalist groups were arrested and killed in cold blood, their houses burnt down and womenfolk raped. Mehraj offered this advice to Kashmiris—"It's much better to strike a deal with the devil than go with Pakistan. Pakistan was trying to project itself as leader of the Muslim world, while at home its forces were committing the genocide of Baloch people, who were Muslims."

My interactions with all these people reaffirmed my faith in India. I felt proud of our visionary leaders who had opted for a secular polity. I took a pledge that I would never ever strike a friendship with a Pakistani and I have kept this promise made to myself.

Here in the UN, I had a deeper understanding of the Pakistani gameplan on Kashmir. Islamabad would train Kashmiri youth in sabotage and terror techniques, who, in turn, would unleash violence back home necessitating a response from the security forces. At this stage, Pakistan would portray the situation as repression of Kashmiris by the Indian Army and also hold it responsible for human rights violations. It was a win-win situation for Islamabad. Besides, the country's omnipotent spy agency, the Inter-Services Intelligence (ISI), had formed a network of people of Kashmiri origin living in the USA and Europe for intensifying propaganda against India in these influential countries. I had met some of them right here in the UN lobby. One of them, Ghulam Nabi Fai, a Kashmir born US citizen, was later sentenced to two years in jail in the USA for receiving funds from the ISI and not disclosing it.

Kashmir was a big talking point at the annual meeting of the UNHRC. Newspapers carried stories about India and Pakistan clashing over Kashmir. Pakistani delegates had the mandate to malign India and tell the world how Muslims were being killed in Kashmir. In the past, New Delhi had sent high profile leaders like Atal Behari Vajpayee and Farooq Abdullah to counter Islamabad. However, overall, Pakistan had managed to create an impression that Indian speakers at the UN meeting were living outside Kashmir and, therefore, had no authority to speak about conditions there. It was true.

On the first day, while moving in the lobby Dr Punjabi had introduced me to a Pakistani delegate. I could see the expression of disbelief on his face as he came to know that I was a Muslim from Srinagar. Pakistanis would generally move around in a group, probably because their government didn't trust them individually or, maybe, they were under instructions to do so. I was told that my presence was a big talking point in the group. They wondered if I was a real Kashmiri. All of them were confused about my identity. I ignored them while moving around and mixing with the delegates of other countries. I could almost feel the piercing gaze of Pakistanis but I learnt to ignore them since it was an opportunity for me to forge work relations with people from around the world. Most delegates were happy to talk to a Kashmiri who was coming straight from Srinagar.

I also visited the library of the United Nations, which is a treasure trove of books and documentation. I can never thank Dr Punjabi enough for taking me under his wing and guiding me. I was supposed to deliver my speech in the UN session after two days. I had a lot to say in my five-minute speech. Dr Punjabi worked with me till late night drafting it. Next day, I spoke of how Pakistan was trying to destroy Kashmir's Islamic syncretism in the name of *jihad*. Pakistani delegates tried to disrupt my speech. One of them even questioned my credentials to speak for the people of Kashmir. However, at the end of my five minutes, the assembly resonated with applause. The UNHRC also took note of my speech; the Indian high commission issued a press handout.

During my twelve day stay in Geneva, the Pakistanis monitored my movements in the lobby. In their narrative, a Kashmiri Muslim living in the Valley should be beholden to them. They considered themselves as the benevolent provider of guns, money and ammunition to the 'poor' Kashmiris to fight

India. Those who rebelled were labelled as *Ikhwanis* or traitors. I had no links with militants and had come from campus politics. Also, I openly prided myself on being an Indian and a follower of Sufi Islam. Pakistanis had never thought that one day they would have to be face to face with such a person from Kashmir. In their minds such people did not exist!

Why were Pakistanis speaking blatant lies at the UN? I realised that Islamabad's mindset on Hindu-Muslim relations was rooted in the partition of India in 1947. Pakistan was created for Muslims while India chose to be a secular nation. In its perception, Pakistan saw India as a Hindu country even though India's Muslim population is more than Pakistan's. In 1971, when Bangladesh was created out of the eastern flank of 'Muslim' Pakistan with India fighting a war with Islamabad, Pakistan was rattled. Its Generals realised that as a smaller 'Muslim' nation, it could never defeat a 'Hindu' army in conventional warfare. So, they opted for a low-cost proxy war against it and chose Kashmir as a battlefield. Pakistan's strategy in launching terrorism and separatist movement in Kashmir was to bog down the Indian Army and security forces in fighting their own people. This was Pakistan's revenge for India's role in creating Bangladesh.

During my career as a political activist, I have realised that Pakistan can never reconcile to its humiliating defeat at the hands of India in the 1971 war in which nearly one lakh Pakistani soldiers were captured as prisoners of war and later returned by a magnanimous victor nation. One wonders how this defeat would have impacted if that too was an era of social media and television boom. Islamabad has always considered 'infidel' India as its key enemy. With rise in Islamic extremism in many parts of the world, it invoked the pride of an Islamic nation befor a *kafir* India. This inevitably led to an upsurge across Pakistan for *jihad* in Kashmir. No wonder hundreds of young Pakistani men volunteered to embrace a sure death by getting enrolled as Pakistan Army's foot soldiers for proxy war-cum-*jihad* in Kashmir.

One day I was introduced to Sartaj Aziz, Pakistan's foreign minister, and a veteran diplomat. Aziz surprised me with his brazen question, "Why are you not siding with Pakistan?" My reply would have been a long explanation but he saved me by not waiting for me to even reply and said, "Independent Kashmir will become a reality in two years; you can become its ambassador to some country."

I politely told him that I had chosen my path; I belonged to India as my culture and civilization were part of the land and its ethos. I told him Kashmiris, like most Indians, believed in tolerance of other faiths and Pakistan's monoculture was alien to them. Later during the session of 2001, three Pakistanis, who looked like officials, walked up to me while I was having coffee in the lobby. One of them said, "What are you doing here? Why are you not fighting for freedom of Kashmir?" His tone was chilling and intimidating.

The problem with Pakistani delegates was that most of them were poor communicators and could barely speak English. They were not confident to approach a foreigner, especially a woman, to strike a conversation.

One day the Muzaffarabad-based Mohammad Safi tried to strike a conversation with me. He was accompanied by three

Punjabi-speaking persons, who looked like ISI officers. He boasted, "We have made the Indian army bow in Kashmir." I was blunt and retorted, "It's a shame for Hurriyat leaders like you to take orders from a defeated army." I was obviously referring to the outcome of the 1971 war.

One day, they sent a Kashmiri terrorist-turned human rights activist to speak with me. He openly threatened me. He told me I should worry about the safety of my family before speaking against Pakistan and *azadi* at Geneva. I was blunt and equally rude to him. I shot back, "How dare you even touch them; just think of Kuka Parray and imagine how he could also harm your family." Parray was a musician turned counter-insurgent fighting for India with guns. The pro-Pakistani terror groups feared him the most.

The Indo-Pak banter at the UN continued for many years until one day the world woke up to Pakistan becoming a state where terrorist leaders like Hafiz Saeed aspired to become the country's rulers.

For the next five years, I would be visiting Geneva twice a year—to attend the annual session of the UNCHR (renamed as United Nations Human Rights Council) and its Sub Commission on the Protection and Promotion of Human Rights. With each visit I was getting insights into Pakistan's gameplan that further made me feel proud of our leaders who threw the lot of Kashmiris with India.

Baptism In Politics

A year after my Geneva visit, the situation in Kashmir took an interesting turn. Hizbul Mujahideen suddenly wanted to give peace a chance. Abdul Majid Dar, a handsome man from north Kashmir, was Hizb's commander for Kashmir. He supervised a protracted and behind the scenes negotiations with intelligence agencies like Intelligence Bureau and the Research and Analysis Wing (RAW), through a group of emissaries. At the end of it, Dar announced a ceasefire after the ISI's approval.

However, since the Kashmir situation has too many control switches, Dar's bold move failed due to a sudden U turn by the Hizb's supreme commander Syed Salahudeen. He had contested elections in 1987 as a candidate for Muslim United Front (MUF) and had lost by a small margin. After Hizb was formed as a pro-Pakistan and Islamic outfit to counter the popular Jammu and Kashmir Liberation Front, Salahudeen walked through north Kashmir's jungles to reach Pakistan occupied Kashmir. There, he was anointed as 'commander in chief' of Hizbul Mujahideen and treated as a guest of the Pakistani establishment. Though Salahudeen and other militants are looked after by the Pakistani authorities, they face curbs on their movements. None of them are allowed to move beyond the territory of the POK and Islamabad-Rawalpindi area. The Hizb chief moves around with a pilot car and a set of personal bodyguards with due protocol generally given to a leader in exile.

Dar continued to hold secret talks with New Delhi's emissaries for nearly a year. During this period, a relative peace had descended across Kashmir and normalcy seemed to be around the corner. He must have made good progress in negotiating the terms of surrender of his men and probably his ambition was soaring. Given the intricacies of the Kashmir situation, Dar was a man probably in a great hurry to see peace return to the Valley. He must have become too big for his boots. In came the hidden hand of Pakistan and suddenly Dar came under pressure to withdraw from negotiations and end the ceasefire. Since Dar wasn't ready to give in so easily, Salahudeen denounced him and expelled him from the Hizb.

In the coming months, Kashmir saw a fresh fratricidal war among the pro-Pakistan militant factions.

In 2002, Abdul Ghani Lone, leader of the All Parties Hurriyat Conference (APHC) was shot in broad daylight right in front of all his colleagues. Lone had finished addressing the public at a rally in Srinagar and was walking towards his seat on the dais when two men fired at him from the front rows of the assembly. Lone collapsed and probably died instantaneously; people were running in all directions, none daring to grab the killers then and there. It was an irony that Lone was killed on a day when he and others were commemorating thc 12th anniversary of the assassination of Moulvi Mohammad Farooq. The Moulvi was killed by an intruder who came to see him in his heavily guarded office on the banks of Nigeen Lake. It was an open secret that both Moulvi Farooq and Lone were killed by Hizbul Mujahideen. The Moulvi was seen as a moderate Kashmiri leader who would never side with Pakistan in case of an eventuality; Lone had taken a position against Islamabad for pushing in foreign mercenaries in Kashmir. Naturally, Pakistan could not trust these men for working for them. Its mandarins feared both Moulvi and Lone were potential challengers for their future strategy on Kashmir. Interestingly, Sayeed Geelani, political patron of Hizbul Mujahideen, had publically shed tears for both slain leaders. Lone's killing caused a lot of squabbling inside the Hurriyat.

A few months later, Abdul Majid Dar was also killed by two unknown gunmen on the outskirts of Sopore. He was supervising construction of his new house when two men trailing him shot him dead.

After his assassination, Abdul Ghani Lone's younger son Sajjad showed tremendous courage by deciding to go it alone in politics. He firmly believed in democracy and elections. He openly said that democracy was the only way to get peoples' aspirations fulfilled. Sajjad happened to be my elder brother's schoolmate in Burn Hall School and they have remained friends till today.

Since I had the experience of managing a students' organisation and also due to our family links, people around me suggested that I join Sajjad's team. At that time, insurgency was at its peak. In fact, Sajjad lived with paradoxes; he distanced himself from his father's last political phase where he was donning the mantle of a separatist and also embraced his political legacy by taking up the challenge to revive the Peoples' Conference, founded by his father. In fact, A G Lone was a self-made man and a moderate politician. At some stage of his political life, he had even favoured removal of Article 370 of the Constitution that confers special powers on the state of J&K. However, in the last phase of his career, he had been subsumed by pro-Pakistan politics and was co-opted in the All Parties Hurriyat Conference (APHC).

The Lone family belonged to Handwara, a quaint town in north Kashmir close to the line of control with Pakistan. Lone was a charismatic leader. No wonder he had the record of never losing an election from Handwara.

After his death, his sons amicably divided their father's legacy; while Bilal chose to be a member of the APHC in place of his father, Sajjad clearly said he couldn't work with those who were silent on his father's killing. He had obviously rejected the Hurriyat Conference.

Violence was at its peak in Kashmir. Under these circumstances, I felt it was quite bold of Sajjad to defy the Hurriyat and take a stand against Pakistan for interfering in Kashmir. Though I had never met him, I used to like his public statements. I met him the first time in his house at Srinagar's Sannat Nagar. A posse of security men on guard duty outside and two Ambassador cars parked inside gave the house the trappings of official power. When I entered his office, Sajjad was busy speaking to a TV channel crew. Indian media had shown interest in him and mostly projected him as a change maker. Sajjad Lone had already been interviewed by the likes of Burkha Dutt, a well known television anchor and journalist.

He warmly hugged me and asked me to wait till he was done with the media. Waiting at his desk, I noticed it looked too organised for a politician's work table. It had exotic and modern stationery including yellow and blue pages for organising notes, and markers of all colours etc. He seemed to be a methodical person and a man of immaculate habits. In his media interactions he came across as an articulate leader. I instantly liked him.

Sajjad asked me to be his political secretary.

My job as Sajjad's political secretary was interesting. Every day, I had to interact with hordes of political workers who came to meet him at his office in Handwara. Many of them were former militants—members of Al Barq—the militant arm of the Peoples' Conference. Back then, as Pakistan's ISI was distributing largesse to Kashmiris who were ready to pick up guns against India, many leaders had floated their own outfits. Some did it purely for pecuniary gains while others didn't want to be left out of the trend. As the visitors waited in my office for their turn to meet Sajjad, many of them chatted with me. Quite often a visitor would speak disapprovingly of Sajjad's choice of a pro-India role and many thought he had betrayed his father. I would be amused to see the same person emerging after his meeting with Sajjad with a calm and happy demeanor.

Sajjad's magic was working; each visitor would come out of his room convinced that he was doing the right thing.

Many visitors' stories were heartrending as not only their dream of *azadi* was nowhere to be realised, their personal lives were shattered. They had been arrested and many had served a prison term. Now, left to fend for themselves they were realising their folly. Most had lost many years of their youth in jail, jeopardised their careers and were now facing acute poverty. Besides, the government authorities showed contempt for ex-militants and treated them shabbily. Sajjad's public statements during campaigning for elections gave them some hope. I was seeing impoverished militants for the first time; so far I had only seen gun-wielding and flamboyant ones. The stereotype of a militant that I had conjured up in my mind turned out to be a myth. These people were desperate and in need of help for personal needs. Most of them had no work, jobs and their families didn't have enough to eat. They would ask Sajjad to help them in starting a small business for livelihood.

Sajjad was slowly emerging as an agent of change. From being seen as the heir to his father's legacy, people had started listening to his developmental narrative. He was becoming a rallying point for all those wanting an end to the violence. Since he was disciplined and hard working, he would even walk 15 km to reach out to the people in hilly hamlets. Mostly his speeches would be around these points: I do understand your agony and hardships caused during years of insurgency and violence. I am not here to sell you dreams of *azadi*; you must know that Pakistan is using us, the people of Kashmir, as pawns in its game against India.

In 2002, Sajjad didn't contest the Assembly election. In fact, he nominated a senior leader of Peoples' Conference, Ghulam Mohiuddin Sofi, as a proxy candidate for Handwara. Sofi, who contested as an independent, won with a decent margin. During the election campaign all PC cadres worked hard to see Sofi win. I guess fielding Sofi was Sajjad's trial balloon; he believed people had validated his peace through development narrative. At the end, Sajjad was confident that the people supported his views.

People had liked Sajjad's brand of clean and honest politics. Many militants who had lost years in jails after being arrested vested their hope in him. They were realising that they had been used and dumped by the pro-Pakistan forces.

Separatist leaders and their masters in Pakistan were aghast at Sajjad's rebellion. Since I was privy to a lot of secret information, I know that many terrorists had been sent to kill Sajjad. His security was routinely reviewed and beefed up.

Sajjad would become emotional while speaking about his father's death. He was angry that none of his father's peers in Hurriyat had even openly condemned his assassins. He would never forget their treachery. Back in those days, he was the first Kashmiri leader to speak openly against the Hurriyat leadership. He would openly call Geelani a liar and accuse him of getting Kashmiris killed for Pakistan's interests. He would even question the credentials of Mirwaiz Moulvi Umer Farooq, another so called moderate leader. "He's not Mirwaiz of Kashmir but of downtown," Sajjad would tell people in public rallies.

With Sajjad, I got to travel across Handwara-Kupwara area

where my father had served for many years. I was building rapport with the locals. Many of them had come to know I was the son of an Indian Army officer; others thought I was an officer of the Intelligence Bureau. Some even considered me as a civil services officer attached to a politician. On my part, I offered no clarification since I was always looking for opportunities to speak to them about ISI's gameplan in Kashmir.

Sajjad Ghani Lone was on the right path of integrating Kashmir with the rest of the country at the emotional level. He continued to work hard with a focus on development and won the 2014 elections to become a minister in the Mehbooba Mufti-led PDP-BJP coalition government.

Sajjad's focus on Kupwara had a ripple effect on the insurgency. Terrorists coming from Pakistan no longer found local support and safe houses in Kupwara and other areas of North Kashmir while returning with bagfuls of grenades, bullets, and Kalashnikovs. Al Barq was disbanded and its cadres had returned home to the People's Conference. Traditionally, north Kashmir was a favourite and easy route for the Kashmiri youth to go to POK, where ISI and Army had opened camps for 'refugees'. After Sajjad's rise, from being a hub of terrorists, north Kashmir had become a peaceful territory.

I firmly believe the credit for this massive change in the ground situation must go to BJP leader Ram Madhav. He had painstakingly worked with the PDP leaders for drafting the agenda of the alliance and sewing this once unthinkable tie-up between PDP and BJP. He liked Sajjad and had mobilised opinion in the party for allocating one ministerial position to him out of party's quota in the J&K government.

Sajjad's foray into politics happened at the right time; people had suffered and were sick of violence; they were looking for a saviour, and, in Sajjad, they had found one. One day we were going for a public rally when a group of villagers intercepted us. They told us that a group of six foreign militants were roaming in a particular village and we must avoid that route. We followed their advice and changed our route. This also meant that they were ready to share information about militants without fear. The Army had launched a massive offensive to mop up residual insurgency in north Kashmir.

People generally realised that insurgency had given them pain and curtailed their freedom of movement; they also considered security forces as their enemies. However, what remained unchanged was their faith in Lone and now in his son. They had followed Abdul Ghani Lone blindly when he wanted their votes and picked up the gun when he asked them to.

As if he was doing penance for his father, Sajjad was on a mission to get his people back into the mainstream. He was smart and his message was clear. He would tell people that Kashmiris were smart enough to decide what was good for them. He would start his interaction with people with a disclaimer, "I am not here to raise emotional slogans and take you down the garden path."

Sajjad told me that he was always against his father's policy of supporting the insurgency. He would caution him that the gun culture he was encouraging would be used to kill the people of Kashmir. Now, after his prophetic fears got his father killed, he would tell people that the only way to reclaim their freedom was to counter the Pakistan-sponsored *jihad*.

I remember an interesting incident of 2004. I am not divulging his identity but he was a vocal legislator in the last Legislative Assembly. The fellow was once caught with a satellite phone and wads of cash that he was carrying in his vehicle for the Lashkar-e-Taiba terrorist group. He was intercepted by the Special Operations group of Police. Since he was a former office bearer of Peoples' Conference, Sajjad Lone had intervened and given a personal undertaking to secure his release.

Sajjad was a rebel with a cause. He would openly own up his cozy relations with the Intelligence Bureau and other central authorities and boisterously say he wanted to become the chief minister one day. To show off his support he had organised the biggest ever public rally in the heart of Srinagar on May 21, 2003, where people raised slogans for peace and against violence and gun culture. That was the last massive public rally held in Srinagar's Sher-e-Kashmir stadium and no political party has been able to match the effort, so far.

Sajjad's brazen admission about his links with Intelligence Bureau and Delhi endeared him to people who saw in him an honest and straightforward leader. His confidence also came from his conviction in his belief that Kashmiris were better off with India.

However, when Congress came to power at the center in 2004, Sajjad lost his support. The government became revengeful. His wife Asma Khan Lone and their twin sons remained stranded in Pakistan for months as the government refused to renew their passports.

I too left that job and returned to journalism in 2006. Within two years, Omar Abdullah had become the chief minister with Congress party's support. Many people of my generation felt disheartened at the return of the National Conference and its leader Farooq Abdullah. Young Kashmiris were angry with Sheikh Mohammad Abdullah for perpetuating the rule of his family and amassing huge wealth. Now not only Farooq had returned to power with a thumping majority but even his son Omar Abdullah had become an MP and a minister a few months later. I am privy to New Delhi's role in manipulating the 1996 elections to give NC an absolute majority in the Legislative Assembly. Instead of taking lessons from the rigged 1987 elections that were always considered a trigger for the insurgency, New Delhi had once again sided with the Abdullahs. In 1996 elections, New Delhi had lost a golden opportunity to prop up and support a new political formation in the state. Ultimately, it happened when the Peoples' Democratic Party was formed by Mufti Mohammad Sayed. He had understood the people's pulse. His mission was denying NC a free run and monopoly, which was a key cause of popular unrest in Kashmir.

The Abdullahs had always sought the support of New Delhi to survive and flourish. The family had kept their interests above that of the people. This made the Kashmiri youth angry. The Abdullahs found a rival in Sajjad Lone and they hated him for getting support from Delhi. Unfortunately, PDP too perpetuated the dynasty when film-maker Tassaduq Mufti was brought in as a backdoor entry into the cabinet by his chief minister sister Mehbooba Mufti. Interestingly, even the Hurriyat Conference is not free from the cult of family rule. So, there is enough reason for New Delhi to change its

Kashmir policy and support independent young leaders to end the rule of a few families and the resultant alienation of people.

In 1996 Abdullah might have returned to power but he did so with embarrassingly low voter turnout. Obviously, people had chosen to remain home than defy militants' diktats of boycott of elections. Abdullah's return to power was not backed by popular will and New Delhi knew this. For this reason, therefore, when Abdullah's government sent the autonomy resolution passed by both the Houses of Legislature to New Delhi, it was duly consigned to the dustbin. Abdullah was back to his party's old ways: he was trying to arouse public sentiments in Kashmir with his demand for autonomy to divert attention from rampant corruption and poor governance that followed. In fact, the 1996 Assembly was held with a larger purpose of countering Pakistan's propaganda about Kashmir. India wanted to show to the world that Kashmir is an integral part of democratic India and what better way to prove it than hold an election.

My Life

In the decade of the nineties, Kashmir was going through unprecedented violence on almost daily basis. Terrorists would throw hand grenades or open fire with Kalashnikovs in marketplaces with the sole purpose of provoking security force personnel standing guard in the mud bunkers on the roadside to retaliate. Invariably, the ensuing clash would take a heavy toll of life—shoppers, students, passers-by, etc. would get caught in the crossfire. Like the scavengers, the Hurriyat leaders seemed be waiting round the corner for people to die for them to emerge and condemn India and the security forces. For them the militants didn't exist in Kashmir so they could do no wrong. None of them had any intention or the will to stop the bloodletting.

So, it was important for the forces to arrest and kill terrorists after smoking them out of the rat holes of hideouts they had built for themselves in the thickly populated quarters of Srinagar city. The terrorists had built secret storages inside houses for piling arms and ammunition brought from Pakistan via Line of Control. Insurgents would take shelter in houses of their supporters and even reluctant hosts in Srinagar city, either for a brief halt or till their plan of attacking security forces was ready to be executed. At times, the information would leak and reach the security forces through informers and even the beat police. The standard operating procedure for the security personnel was to plan a cordon and search operation (CASO) of the general area where the terrorists would be hiding. Interestingly, people called the pre-dawn exercise as 'crackdown'. It would start with a sudden announcement by Force personnel from hand-held megaphones or at times through the public address systems of mosques calling people—men, women, and children—to come out and assemble in a designated open space. The soldiers would carry out house to house search for arms and latent terrorists.

In another dramatic ritual of the CASO all men would be asked to face a bullet-proof vehicle that had its windshield covered with iron mesh, possibly to ward off an attack. A masked man sitting behind the wheel would tell a terrorist or an active supporter of terrorist outfits from an innocent person. People feared this parade as one nod from the masked man could send them to a virtual hell. The man inside the vehicle would either be an informer who had tipped the authorities about what they were looking for—terrorists, their logistic managers and hidden arms. As and when he nodded his head, the person would be quickly rounded up then and there and sent to an interrogation center like Papa 2 or Papa 1, our own little Guantanamo Bays.

During my college days, I was living in a rented house in Rajbagh, Srinagar. Early one morning, I also heard the call for the residents to come out and assemble in a nearby ground; we were under crackdown. During the routine drill, the army officers would deliberately tend to communicate with young persons. An officer in his thirties asked me to show him around while he continued his conversation with me. I could make out that he was a South Indian and held the rank of a Major. He appeared to be friendly. I told him that I too wanted to join the Army. He asked me to meet him at his unit in Zakura on Srinagar outskirts and also gave me a landline contact number. He was part of the 17 Infantry Brigade of the Indian Army.

One day, he invited me to Zakura to meet his commander Brigadier Shivrein. At the outset when the Brigadier asked me about my family and I told him about my father, he almost jumped out of the chair. He had worked under him. He was very eager to see my father and he came over to our house in Ganderbal. At Zakura, I was treated like an important guest, served tea and snacks over a cozy conversation with the commander.

The Major and I remained friends long after he had been posted out of Kashmir. In 2011, he invited me over to Delhi for a wedding in his wife's family. Little did I know that this visit would change my life!

In Delhi at the wedding reception, the Major introduced me to his family and relatives. Everyone behaved normally with me and treated me well. Honestly, back then, visiting outside

Kashmir was scary for young Kashmiris, for everyone looked at us with hostility and treated us as enemies. Kashmiri Muslims didn't even get rented accommodation or a room in a hotel those days.

My Major friend had introduced me to his cousin Susan. She was a student of Electronic Engineering in Coimbatore, Tamil Nadu. Dressed in a sari and wearing strands of jasmine flowers in her hair, Susan came across as a simple and confident young lady. At the function, we chatted and ended up exchanging our email addresses. We would communicate through yahoo messenger and even telephone calls stretching into sixty minutes or so.

Interaction with Susan had filled me with positivity and optimism. Coming from Kashmir, where pessimism and gloom ruled our lives, it was but natural for me to think that this woman had magical powers.

By now, I knew a lot about Susan. She belonged to a mixed Tamil family—her father was a Roman Catholic and mother a devout Hindu, Brahmin by caste, from the city of Thanjavur. She prayed in temples and the church and she was a vegetarian. Her father was a businessman and most of her relatives lived abroad in Europe and Australia.

Susan was raised with belief in the power of religion, especially prayers; yet she held a secular outlook towards others. This was my first encounter with families with secular beliefs. Each member of this family was deeply religious and yet respected other faiths. This was close to my dream world, the contours of which had been shaped by my secular-minded father.

In 2001, I visited Coimbatore with my friends to meet Susan. It was my first visit to South India. Coimbatore looked lovely with its greenery and hills and happy faces all around. Susan came with her brood of friends and met me in a restaurant called *Gauri Shankar* where I ate a dosa for the first time. I took an instant liking to south Indian filter coffee. We all went for a movie. Susan was riding a scooter and I was her pillion rider.

We soon decided to get married.

The first person I chose to inform about this was my father. Expectedly, he was happy and gave me the go-ahead. Like most other societies, Kashmir is a male-dominated one. The opinion of male members matters more, and hence the murmurs of disapproval coming from my mother and sister really didn't matter. However, my family had fears about the feasibility of a distant marriage. Would it be possible for us—separated by 2000 km, religion and culture—to make our marriage a success?

I was sure I wanted to marry Susan and become part of the cultural milieu that she came from. Her mother would pray in the temple and also visit the church. There was so much harmony around that I found was missing in my place. All these thoughts crossed my mind while I was thinking of Susan.

Susan faced an even bigger challenge with her relatives. Her uncles (mother's brothers) had a major say in her choice of a partner. They detested the idea of their niece marrying a Kashmiri Muslim. They also believed that all Muslims were poor and backward. However, my Army friend and Susan's cousin played a key role in making the family pay a visit to Kashmir to see for themselves how well most of the Kashmiri

Muslims lived. The family paid a secret visit to Kashmir and even saw my house from a distance. After this the *mamas* softened their stand.

Finally, a group of twelve members from Kashmir reached Thanjavur in June 2002 for our wedding. Susan's family had arranged for our stay in a hotel. This came as a cultural shock to many as Kashmiris generally welcome the *baratis* at their own homes. Interestingly, some of the guests started getting paranoid suspecting this might be a trap and soon they would be arrested by the police because of the inter-faith wedding that we had come for. However, it turned out that Susan's family believed in the Hindu ritual of doing important things at the pre-decided auspicious time called *Muhurat*. They wanted their daughter's future in-laws to enter their house at a fixed moment that was decided by the priests after making calculations about her birth time and mine.

SOLEMNISING THE WEDDING

I entered Susan's home along with my family and friends at a given time. Interesting rituals followed which none of us had seen before. I was made to stand on a beautifully designed Rangoli and Susan's mother welcomed me with an *aarti thali*. This was a touching moment for me. I had to break a coconut to enter the house. I was offered milk in a silver tumbler to drink.

Thereafter, I was taken to the puja room for prayers. Pictures of Hindu Gods and Goddesses and Jesus Christ adorned the walls. This was amazing for me. After our wedding, a picture of Kashmir's Hazratbal shrine, where a relic of Prophet

Mohammad is kept, has been added to the celestial symbols in the puja room.

We were served biryani on banana leaves. Again, this was a cultural shock for Kashmiris, many of whom took it as an insult. My friends simply told me they didn't like the food. They also didn't appreciate Susan's looks. One of my cousin's remarked, "I thought you were marrying an English woman." He and others had a stereotyped image of a Christian in their minds and they believed all Christians are either Europeans or Americans. Even my mother was not very pleased with the bride's looks as she could not look beyond the colour of her skin that was nowhere near the complexion she was used to seeing around her.

I was very engrossed in watching the coconut breaking ceremony as we entered a temple for our wedding ceremony. I wore the traditional south Indian dress—lungi—for our temple wedding. Later, we also visited the Church where the whole family prayed together.

At Thanjavur, Susan's *mama* had a reception in a local temple for us. There I found myself partaking food with all the Brahmins and temple priests inside the temple premises. Everyone showed deep respect for the son-in-law. It was again a very touching moment for me as her uncle who had opposed our wedding hosted the luncheon in the temple. In Kashmir, we were given to believe that Hindus don't allow Muslims to touch their food leave alone being allowed to enter their temples and shrines. Here, I was being served food inside the temple along with the priests. All through the ceremonies and the following celebrations, I kept thinking about the great things that India stands for. The rich traditions, the faith, the culture of the people is so varied and yet at a human level everyone is the same. Traditions like respect for a son-in-law, love for the outsiders once they decide to connect is common to all cultures. It was my first exposure to traditional Hindu culture.

The wedding party stayed there for ten days and we went around Ooty and other places before returning home to Kashmir.

At home, my uncle had taken charge. As soon as I arrived he had arranged a maulvi Sahib to perform our *nikah*. Susan had no problems with this. My uncles had picked a Muslim sounding name for Susan and were suggesting she be converted to Islam. Religion had never come in the way of our togetherness and I frankly didn't know how to handle it at that time. Mercifully, my father put his foot down on religious conversion and even a change of name for Susan. Taken aback, the maulvi sahib told everyone that there is a provision of inter-faith marriage among the people of the books—*Ahle Kitab*—a loose reference to the common origins of Semitic religions of Judaism and Christianity. Such a marriage was permitted. Susan was a devout and practising Christian and she felt happy that nobody was snatching her faith from her. I always thank God for saving me from this difficult situation.

Susan instantly liked Kashmir. Ours was a unique marriage celebrated openly. Back in those days, a lot of top leaders fell for Pakistani women since Kashmir was passing through a turmoil and normal interaction between the two sexes was minimal; finding a match for eligible boys and girls was becoming difficult for parents. Back then, leaders like Omar Abdullah had married a Hindu woman from Haryana and Yasin Malik and Sajjad Lone had married Pakistanis.

At one point it was also a clash of religious ideologies in Kashmir and weddings like ours did help change the discourse. After our wedding, my friends and cousins started thinking that India wasn't a hostile place; they thought if Khalid can get married to a woman of another faith with the consent of her family, they too could venture to explore life around in the bigger world that India offered them.

Susan's first winter wasn't easy. Interestingly, now she finds the weather in Kashmir the best part of her life. Otherwise, she tried to adapt fast to the new place and culture. I always knew women are good at this. Though people at my home didn't dislike Susan but there is a limit to which young inter-faith couples can live in joint families. I felt there was subtle hostility for the outsider and its continuation would make our life difficult. We decided to shift to Srinagar and live as a nuclear family.

I had to shelve my plans for political activism and take up a journalistic assignment to make both ends meet. Susan got a job in Burn Hall School, my alma mater. After a year, our first daughter Sofia was born at Coimbatore. Susan had to follow the south Indian tradition of delivering her first child at her parent's place. Life wasn't a bed of roses. Susan returned to her job and she would return by 2 pm.

I would babysit Sofia till she returned. Susan brought a lot of stability in my life. One thing that I have learned from her is that one should never give up one's faith and one should have faith in the power of prayers.

Sofia is today studying in the 8th standard and our second daughter Rania is eight-years-old. Needless to say, Tamil language and food dominates our home. The girls have become polyglots; they speak Tamil with their Mom, Hindi or English with me and Kashmiri with their *dadimaa*, their grandmother. They have also learned Arabic by recitation of *Quran*. The girls have read the Bible and are now reading *Mahabharata* too. As a family we visit temples and churches together. Both my daughters love the Kashmiri ritual of distributing yellow rice at the mausoleum of Sufi saints. Whenever we visit Ganderbal both Rania and Sofia insist on visiting the shrine of Qamar sahib.

In some ways, Susan is more of a Kashmiri than all of us. She loves the weather and now when she has to go to the South, she finds the heat unbearable and wants to return home at the earliest. She speaks all good things about Kashmir and its people. In that sense she is an undesignated ambassador of Kashmir. In fact, she had received great job offers from abroad but she preferred her present job saying that she loves being in touch with Kashmiris. A low key person, Susan works as an administrator in Burn Hall. She has a bigger outreach to the people than me. She even counsels students who get misled by the propaganda around and is involved in a lot of social and community work.

Today, I feel so blessed to know that there are so many people of different faiths in my life; each one praying for me. My mother-in-law holds a special puja for me every month in a temple in Thanjavur. It's a great feeling to know that someone sitting thousands of miles away is praying for your welfare. It surely helps. I am treated like a VVIP whenever I visit Susan's family and, frankly, I have started enjoying my few days of 'royal treatment'.

After my marriage, I thought it was important for me to know more about the South and its people. The best way to do it in India is going on a train journey. I took the train from Delhi to Chennai and further travelled to Velankanni, Madurai, Tiruchirappalli, Ooty, Wellington, Kodaikanal, and the Balaji temple at Tirupati.

I am fascinated by the rich cultural traditions and simplicity of life across Tamil Nadu and rest of the south. People don't believe in showing off, are God-fearing and deeply religious. Inside homes, they live simple lives. The first time I saw Susan's father sleep on a mat on the bare floor/I was surprised. Later, even I liked wearing a lungi and sleeping on the floor.

Today, as a Kashmiri with a second home in Coimbatore, I feel blessed.

Media And Politics

After my brief stint with Sajjad Lone, I wanted to do more interesting work. In the meanwhile, the National Conference government headed by Omar Abdullah had taken charge and Sajjad's initiatives were not getting support from the government. Besides, I was looking for a job that would give me a regular income to take care of Susan and my first born. A regular job would also give me a standing in the society. Like most young persons, I was under a kind of indirect pressure from the family and relatives to 'settle down'. In Kashmir, one becomes socially relevant and acceptable only after a government job. Since I had worked with Sajjad Lone while he still carried the label of being a separatist, I knew I had no chance of getting into the government.

Those days, a young Kashmiri journalist Shujaat Bukhari had launched an English newspaper—*Rising Kashmir*. The newspaper was still at the dummy stage. I was fascinated by its young owner Shujaat who had quit his job with *The Hindu* newspaper to launch his enterprise—as I was with the idea of a professionally managed English newspaper being launched in Kashmir. I joined its editorial team in early 2008.

The launch of *Rising Kashmir* was a great phenomenon. Till that time, journalism was seen as the last resort of all those who had failed in life. Bukhari's newspaper and his rise came as a ray of hope for the youngsters in more ways than one. Bukhari didn't belong to a powerful dynasty or a clan; he had worked as a reporter from Srinagar for one of India's most reputed newspaper groups. He had hired some of the finest minds from Delhi newsrooms to help train his team and shape his newspaper. For us, each day would be a learning experience. The team was gaining confidence and just three months before the Amarnath land row had spluttered into a massive agitation, *Rising Kashmir* was on the newsstands across the state.

Another reason why Shujaat Bukhari's newspaper became a rage and a harbinger of hope was because he was a self-made man and therefore the younger generation saw in him a role model. Kashmiris had been pushed into a system where they believed that merit and enterprise have no value; connections, especially with politicians and their stooges, do. A sense of pessimism hung around and, therefore, amidst this Shujaat's rise was a welcome change and he became a trendsetter.

From day one, *Rising Kashmir* was a rousing success. The younger generation of Kashmiris had lapped it up as a modern and first English newspaper from Kashmir which not only gave space to Kashmir-centric issues and their aspirations but also created a springboard for budding journalists and their careers. Many journalists who had taken baby steps in *Rising Kashmir*, have moved up in life and are working with national and international media institutions. It sounds awkward, but I must admit that the Amarnath agitation gave a major boost to the circulation of *Rising Kashmir*. The newspaper had started publication three months before the agitation had brought life in Kashmir to a screeching halt. In the newsroom, every day, we would work hard to bring out the next day's paper with perfection. We took special care to give a balanced coverage of what had essentially evolved as a Hindu versus Muslim and Jammu versus Kashmir agitation. In both the regions of the state—Kashmir and Jammu—people were up in arms and on the roads for different and conflicting reasons.

In Kashmir, people were on the warpath with the government because they thought it had given away forest land for construction of buildings and other infrastructure to facilitate the pilgrimage to the holy cave of Lord Shiva at Amarnath. Syed Ali Shah Geelani and his peers spread stories that the buildings en route the glacial cave of Lord Shiva, that opens for pilgrims for a month during July-August , was ultimately meant to be used for settling Hindus from outside to change the Muslim-majority character of Kashmir. People were taken in by this. On the other hand, people in Jammu were angry and shut down work and businesses for a month in anger against Kashmiri Muslims objecting to an ancient Hindu pilgrimage. Jammu and Kashmir had plunged into chaos as Congress Chief Minister Ghulam Nabi Azad resigned as its ally the Peoples Democratic Party (PDP) withdrew support. That was a difficult period for reporters especially those who were consciously trying not to inflame the situation further.

Rising Kashmir was attracting readers and the revenue from advertisements was rising steadily. The newspaper became a success story within months of its inception. Back then, another English daily *Greater Kashmir* was already established, but with *Rising Kashmir's* sudden and quick growth, its owner Fayaz Ahmad Kaloo had to pull up his socks and brace for the competition. Many would, however, wonder why this thirst for English language newspapers in Kashmir? They must understand that being a great dateline Kashmir always generated news and naturally its people were news hungry. The irony was that due to poor transportation facilities, English newspapers from Jammu and Delhi would arrive in Srinagar only in the evening. In smaller towns, the newspaper would be carried by road and readers would be able to read it only the next day. In winter, when road and air links to Kashmir got snapped for days, the newspapers would arrive much later. The advent of *Greater Kashmir* and *Rising Kashmir* changed this trend; the news-hungry and globalized generation of Kashmir lapped up the twin English newspapers as these were delivered early morning.

After about one-and-a-half years, I received an interesting job offer. The Delhi-based *Political and Business Daily* became the first national daily to start an edition from Srinagar. I became its resident editor. By now Omar Abdullah had become chief minister due to a huge anti-PDP wave in the wake of the Amarnath agitation and the resultant violence. The edition was launched with a lot of fanfare with important persons like Vice

Chancellor of the Islamic University Sadiq Wahid, J&K Bank Chairperson Haseeb Drabu, Editor, *Srinagar Times* and famous cartoonist Bashir Ahmed Bashir who is more famous as BAB the cartoonist, Shujaat Bukhari, Director J&K Cultural Academy Zafar Manhas attending the function at the Broadway hotel.

Four years later, I landed a prestigious job as India correspondent of the UK-based *Channel Four Television*, and also had an assignment with a German television *ARD*. I was active in media and was nominated as president of Indian Federation of Working Journalists (IFWJ) that was once headed by legendary Pran Nath Jalali.

Due to international assignments, I got to travel to global conflict spots like Iraq and Afghanistan and also across many Muslim societies. During these visits, I could understand the wider and long-term implications of terrorism on societies. I saw the devastation that terrorism and religious extremism had caused to nations and the once great civilizations. I also got involved in a couple of think tanks engaged in fighting the basic ideology behind terrorism. These activities helped me understand the global scene.

Those days, the scenario of Kashmir media was interesting. There were very few genuine and qualified professionals around. Most of those masquerading as journalists were associated with a political or ideological group. Many worked as public relations agents of politicians. Some worked rather openly for the separatist conglomerate Hurriyat Conference; a few for CID, the police department that gathers political intelligence for the government in power. Another group of journalists were on the payroll of wealthy, yet not much known politicians.

They behaved like agents of their masters and whenever they got a chance, they would project them through the newspaper columns. Journalists received abysmally low salaries. For this reason, many felt no guilt while receiving stipends from the politician they had agreed to work for. After all, they had to make both ends meet. On the other hand, as insurgency and violence raged, many young journalists would fashion their talk and news coverage as if they were covering the Israeli-Palestine conflict in Gaza. Kashmir media was turning into a theatre of the bizarre!

A generation of professional journalists should be grateful to Kaloo and Bukhari for creating platforms and giving them opportunities for a career.

In the middle of writing this book, I was shattered to hear about the assassination of Shujaat Bukhari. Three days before he was killed by terrorists we had met on the lawns of Srinagar's Raj Bhawan, where Governor N N Vohra had hosted an Iftaar party for politicians and journalists. Shujaat was not given to mincing his words; he told me point blank that BJP had betrayed the people of Kashmir. He alleged that BJP, as part of the government, had failed to give good governance to people. He even told me that while young activists like me had opted for mainstream political parties, the situation remained unchanged in Kashmir. I remember like a true well-wisher Shujaat had advised me to take care of my personal safety as terrorists would like to target me. His concern was of a friend who had seen me in my struggling phase.

Earlier, when US diplomat Lisa Curtis visited Kashmir in 2017, she had met Bukhari. He passionately discussed why the interests of the people of Kashmir should be the peg around which the resolution about Kashmir should be drafted. He told her that India and Pakistan must become friends for bringing peace to Kashmir. Shujaat was also concerned about growing incidents of terrorism in the valley.

During our interactions, Shujaat would always wonder why Delhi would not talk to Mirwaiz Maulvi Umar Farooq. The young Maulvi was pitchforked into clergyship and politics of secession under tragic circumstances—his father Maulvi Farooq was killed by a Hizbul mujahideen terrorist on Pakistan's orders. Being the youngest of the Hurriyat leaders, he would be yearning for peace. Shujaat always felt that Mirwaiz was the best bet for India to talk to; at least he would like Kashmir to be peaceful for the sake of his young children. Unlike SAS Geelani, who, at an advanced age had no inclination for peace as he wanted to be remembered as a pro-Pakistan and Islamist protagonist, Mirwaiz had interest in normalcy. I have a strong feeling that Bukhari was killed because he was lobbying with New Delhi for initiating talks with Mirwaiz.

While working for television, I made a documentary on the life of people living inside Srinagar's Dal Lake for Dog Haus—a German production house. The documentary was shown in the Berlin Film Festival. I was enjoying myself as my work was getting attention. I also covered the phenomenon of youth with stones in their hands taking on the security forces on the roads of Srinagar and other towns of the Valley for at least five months. There was no doubt about the fact that the stone pelting was sponsored by Pakistan since it had interest in keeping the pot boiling in Kashmir. I also reported cases of excesses by the Army during counter-insurgency operations.

Due to my years of activism in college, I was keen to be a change-maker. The only way to do this in Kashmir was by joining a political party. From my experience with them, I found that Kashmiri politicians are the most arrogant in the country; they throw tantrums and can snub even the most powerful bureaucrats and top-ranking journalists. Manned by such leaders, no political party had an opening for a newcomer who didn't come from an influential political family.

It's tragic to see how established politicians across the parties only encouraged the children and relatives of former ministers, leaders and other senior activists. The trend was common to all the parties. Mufti Mohammad Sayeed had picked his daughter Mehbooba Mufti when he decided to break free of Congress and launch his outfit. In turn, Mehbooba coaxed her film-maker brother Tassaduq Mufti to join her when the going got tough for her.

About National Conference, the less said the better. The party, like Congress at the center, is headed by a third generation of the Sheikhs. Even NC-turned-Congress leader Saifuddin Soz brought his MNC executive son Salman Soz from the Gulf to join Congress. Overnight, Salman became a national spokesperson of the Indian National Congress in Delhi as if he had an organic link with India's oldest political party. Likewise, all the senior leaders have managed entry and positions for their scions and relatives in their respective parties.

In fact, people generally believed Farooq Abdullah would not bring his son Omar into politics since by that time Kashmir had seen bloodshed and unrest. Besides historical factors, a strong anti-Abdullah family sentiment had also contributed to the unrest. However, he did call his son from London to take over NC's reins. Omar was straightaway made to contest for Lok Sabha. Omar is the only son of Farooq Abdullah. He and his British wife Molly have three daughters. He had studied in Sanawar School in Himachal Pradesh and later in Maharashtra. He couldn't speak a word of Kashmiri and yet he confidently entered a party which was seething with 'Kashmiri' sub-nationalism. Sheikh Mohammad Abdullah's grandson took over the reins of his party and people. Yet again, I realised that there was no entry for common people in politics on merit. The bloodline counts when it comes to leadership.

In Kashmir's political arena, leaders didn't even make a pretense of proving the old age adage 'blood is thicker than water', wrong. This is one of the fundamental causes for the rage of youth in Kashmir.

THE HURRIYAT: LOST OPPORTUNITY

The sudden emergence of All Parties Hurriyat Conference (APHC) in 1993—four years after insurgency started—offered another opportunity to young people to join politics. The rush for joining Hurriyat was in spite of people realising that Hurriyat Conference had been cobbled on orders of Pakistan. At a time when militant groups seemed to be indulging in unpopular actions and were losing support, Islamabad wanted a political front to support and speak for them. Many of the gunmen had lost the initial zeal and sense of purpose and had turned extortionists, killers, looters; they were victimising the upper-middle-class families.

Pakistan's Kashmir-managers must have realised that the gun alone formula was not working on the ground; also, it was giving a bad name to the Kashmir movement. So they decided to create a political umbrella whose leaders would be able to speak up for Kashmir's cause in political terms. The APHC was put together out of leaders of smaller parties with anti-India tendencies. Abdul Gani Lone was, in fact, the architect of the Hurriyat; he was instrumental in purchasing the building in Srinagar's Raj Bagh where the Hurriyat office is located. The task of Hurriyat leaders was to fashion the armed movement and political discourse along Islamic lines. Religion is such a potent force in South Asia that both Pakistanis and their Kashmiri allies agreed on using religion for bringing in cohesion in the 'movement'.

For me, APHC was not an option since it was a Pakistan-sponsored group. Its leaders pursued the same old policies. They were trying to legitimise Pakistan's claim on Jammu and Kashmir. The day Pakistan had sidelined the JKLF and introduced the Hizbul Mujahideen in Kashmir, it had killed the idea of independence or *azadi*. The conglomerate was directly controlled by Islamabad. Gradually, the inherent differences within the group started to emerge and one day it split into two—one faction of hardliners was led by Sayed Ali Shah Geelani and the other—of the moderates—by Mirwaiz Maulvi Umar Farooq.

Thus APHC was launched to project Kashmir's struggle as an indigenous one and not sponsored by Islamabad. Thus, Hurriyat had helped Pakistan carry out its proxy war against India to avenge creation of Bangladesh and keep its claim on

Kashmir alive. Today in 2019, all factions of APHC continue to support Pakistan's narrative of Kashmir being an unfinished agenda of the partition. To Islamabad's chagrin, till now no other nation has supported this contention. Instead of playing a positive role in changing the situation in Kashmir, the leaders of Hurriyat continue to create a negative image of the Indian state in Kashmir. They successfully mobilise public opinion against the Indian state and label political leaders, the government of India, its Prime Minister and the Armed Forces as aggressors and violators of human rights. In fact, Hurriyat leaders had a great chance to bring about a change in Kashmir, but its leaders chose to play into Pakistan's hands even if it caused a lot of bloodletting in Kashmir. Instead of steering Kashmiris' legitimate grievances in a meaningful direction, these leaders chose to become propaganda machines for Pakistan. They issued statements that were endorsed by their masters sitting in Rawalpindi, the headquarters of ISI and Pakistan Army.

Even after three decades of pain and agony inflicted upon the people of Kashmir, these leaders continue to harp on the same narratives that one heard from a handful of people in 1947, around the time of partition. Leaders like Fazul Haque Qureshi, etc. who rebelled against *jihad* elements being introduced in Kashmir were done to death. We also realised that most of the APHC leaders enjoyed proximity to the ministers and bureaucrats and their kith and kin were given plum positions, jobs and government contracts on a priority basis. I am privy to many instances where the chief minister was in touch with Hurriyat leaders through back channels. That way regional political parties and Hurriyat were working in tandem to weaken the national cause. They tied people in knots by floating slogans about *azadi*, Pakistan, *jihad*, autonomy, self-rule etc.

Hurriyat leaders lived double lives; some of them were secretly selling medical seats in Pakistani colleges to Kashmiri students while enjoying a protective cover of Z category offered by the Indian establishment. Hurriyat leaders almost ran a parallel government in Kashmir. However, in the public domain they remained under house arrest and were prevented from marching on roads. This was a convenient cover for their families to enjoy a luxurious life outside Kashmir and their children to study abroad. The leaders took breaks in Delhi, Islamabad, Dubai and other countries.

In fact, Hurriyat turned out to be yet another group that perpetuated dynastic rule; its leadership has no young faces. Hurriyat has failed Kashmiri youth, who were angry at New Delhi for pampering a few chosen families and had opted to support the idea of freedom or *azadi*. Hurriyat was trying to lead them to Pakistan, not their original dream. The fact that Kashmiris—policemen, intelligence agencies and common people who extracted and fed information about presence of terrorists to the combat forces—are today in the forefront of battling terrorism sponsored by Pakistan is a signal that there is no love lost for Pakistan in Kashmir.

NEW EXPERIENCE

While working for German Radio, I would often visit the BJP headquarters at New Delhi's Ashoka Road to get quotes of the party leaders for my stories. Ravi Shankar Prasad was the party spokesperson those days and he was available all the time. I would also get to meet Ram Madhav, spokesperson, Rashtriya Swayamsevak Sangh (RSS). They would exude warmth and speak openly on issues that I either wanted to understand from BJP's perspective or get their opinion on. At times, I would get invited to Ravi Shankar Prasad's home for a sound byte. He would never get irritated or try to avoid me. It was a new experience for me as back home, most leaders are arrogant to the core and journalists can't even dream of getting an appointment with them. Even bureaucrats have adopted this style. They never pick up their phones leave alone returning the call of a journalist. Most of them would discuss global issues and even have solutions for them but they never cared for the people they were appointed to serve. In Kashmir, legislators and ministers had won elections by a margin of fewer than 1,000 votes (since polling percentage was very low), yet they had no qualms in calling themselves mass leaders.

The experience of covering BJP came like a whiff of fresh air to me. One day, when I went to Ravi Shankarji's house he introduced me to his family and also offered me food. Honestly, contrary to the fears that most Kashmiri Muslims have about BJP, they never made me feel I was any different. The first time I went to BJP headquarters, I was accompanied by a Kashmiri businessman friend of mine who lived in Delhi's Lajpat Nagar. He was scared to enter the office and told me that the 'sanghis' would kill us. He had me scared.

My bonding with BJP leaders transcended the neta-journalist relation as they would speak with me about Kashmir situation with interest. I was once treated to a dosa at Ravi

Shankar Prasad's house located at Mother Teresa road in Delhi. I started reading about BJP, its ideology and history, and found BJP was the only party that had not used and dumped Kashmiris.

At that time BJP was in opposition and yet the leaders maintained their links with me. Whenever the graph of violence in Kashmir went up they would call me and others and ask for suggestions.

While I was in Delhi I realised the duplicity and hypocrisy of Kashmiri leaders including the separatists. In the Valley, they spit fire against the central leadership and keep calling BJP and Congress *Qatil* (killers) of Kashmiris, while in Delhi they meet political leaders and seek personal favours. It dawned upon me that Kashmiris had been deliberately fed with hate and propaganda against Delhi by the regional parties and the Hurriyat leaders. Why should we, the Kashmiris, not be in direct touch with Delhi? Why not join a national party? Congress again was a dynastic party and it didn't appeal to me for obvious reasons.

BJP seemed to be the best option for Kashmir.

If after Jawahar Lal Nehru and Indira Gandhi there is any leader who is liked by Kashmiri people, it's the former Prime Minister Atal Behari Vajpayee. His name still stirs Kashmiris' souls and rekindles hope. He gets credit for inserting the word *insaniyat* (humanity) in the lexicon on reconciliation of Kashmir. There is a lot of misinformation about Vajpayee's *insaniyat* remark and I find it funny when even BJP leaders don't get it right. Here is the correct version: One day when Prime Minister Vajpayee was visiting Kashmir he told mediapersons that BJP government would talk to the militants. At this a reporter asked him, "*Kya baatcheet* Constitution *ke dayre mein hogi* (Would you hold the proposed talks within the ambit of the Constitution)?" He replied without batting an eyelid, "*Baatcheet insaniyat ke dayre mein hogi* (the talks will be held under the aegis of humanity)."

The scribe had asked a tricky question; Vajpayee's reply floored everyone. Since then, *Insaniyat* has become a popular tagline for any talk about reconciliation in Kashmir. It's a convenient term for everyone—people, leaders and New Delhi alike—to start a conversation and move away from their hard-line positions on Kashmir.

As against BJP's approach, Congress has been responsible for all the ills troubling Kashmir. The party is hugely responsible for eroding the economy of the state. When I was growing up in Kashmir it was probably hard for us to see through the game of Kashmiri leaders to keep the people away from Delhi. However, today's younger generation, empowered as it is with the surfeit of information and perspective through social media etc. are certainly in a better position to make discerning choices.

I was clearly leaning towards the BJP.

Joining BJP

The Amarnath agitations across Kashmir Valley and Jammu further exacerbated the situation in the State. As the government was trying to deal with mass protests in Kashmir, quite unexpectedly, Jammu rose in anger against the protests in Kashmir. Ghulam Nabi Azad's government fell as PDP withdrew support to the coalition arrangement. The two parties had sewn a coalition and agreed to take turns to head the government. This agreement saw Mufti Mohammad Sayeed as chief minister for the first three years. In June 2005, it was the turn of Congress to take charge of the government. The party lacked a tall leader and it had to coax one of its veterans in Delhi to fly to Srinagar for heading the government in J&K. Azad was a son of the soil—he hailed from the mountainous district of Doda. He had mostly played his innings in Congress outside the state. He was considered as an ace negotiator and loyalist of the Nehru-Gandhi family and had won the award for best parliamentarian many a time.

However, Azad had never shown inclination for a role in his home state. Reluctantly, he had come to Kashmir to be anointed as chief minister—something that was not exactly his perception of promotion. His term was coming to an end when a major controversy erupted over his government's 'decision' to hand over swathes of forest land to the Amarnath Shrine Board that looks after the annual pilgrimage. The land was supposed to be used for setting up facilities for the pilgrims. Azad later claimed the decision was a routine one. The cabinet meeting that took the decision to hand over the land to the shrine board was also attended by PDP ministers and it was not a hush-hush decision. However, much later, when the separatists got a whiff of it and they projected it as a diabolical ploy of the government to settle non-local Hindus in Kashmir on this land, PDP chief Mehbooba Mufti suddenly did a U-turn and sided with the protesters. The reality was that the land had not been handed over to the Shrine board. On hearing the news about widespread protests, Mehbooba air dashed to Srinagar, where Azad was waiting for her. He wanted to speak with her but she had already made up her mind. She asked the PDP to pull the rug from under Azad's feet by withdrawing its support to his government leaving the veteran leader red-faced.

PDP's act emboldened the separatists; it was a clear validation of their stand that the real purpose of the land transfer order was to eventually settle Hindus from the mainland. Their assessment was that since New Delhi was desperate for a resolution of the Kashmir issue, one of the ways to do so was to change the Muslim majority character of the Valley. For this, the separatists feared the government would bring in and settle outsiders.

People in Kashmir generally tend to believe conspiracy theories, even bizarre ones; in particular, those in which New Delhi figures as a villain. People easily believed that the Azad government was hand in glove with New Delhi for the sinister plan. They were told that the purported grabbing of the forest land was an idea of Governor S K Sinha, a former Army General, who headed the Amarnath Shrine Board. Sinha had already annoyed separatists by ordering the University of Kashmir and many colleges to hold seminars and debates on topic of Sufism at a time when the separatists were trying to impose a radical form of Islam in Kashmir. The PDP had played a political game by projecting itself as a watchdog of the interests of Kashmiri Muslims and Congress as the agent of New Delhi. No wonder, this plot unfolded in the nick of time as elections were just a few months away.

The region of Jammu had been peaceful all these years of insurgency and unrest in Kashmir. However, this time it had erupted in anger over the Amarnath issue. People here felt that the Kashmiri Muslims were against Hindu pilgrimage and Muslim leaders in the government were supporting them. Jammu had never seen an agitation of this nature and magnitude before.

In the summer of 2008, when tumultuous events were unfolding in J&K, BJP was in the opposition in the center. Its leaders would call me often to check the facts about daily events. They probably chose me so that they could get a true picture of the situation and not fall prey to the propaganda and rumours. Since the party's legislators and most of the leaders belonged to Jammu, they might present a one-sided picture to them. The BJP leaders in Delhi, therefore, banked on me for an accurate picture of the Valley so that they could make an objective assessment and have a comprehensive view. At that time, Narendra Modi was Chief Minister of Gujarat. I would get calls from his office and from other BJP leaders from Gujarat too. From Delhi, Ravi Shankar Prasad and Ram Madhav would regularly call me. BJP's interest in Kashmir was intriguing; the party was virtually non-existent here yet its leaders kept tabs on the situation. I was amazed to see the level of interest the party leaders showed in the agitation and emerging scenarios in both the regions.

In the meanwhile, the movement for a Lok Pal Bill by Anna Hazare had given birth to a new political party—Aam Aadmi Party (AAP). This new party was led by a former bureaucrat Arvind Kejriwal who went on to win a landslide victory in the elections and form a government in Delhi. AAP's rise had fired the imagination of many young Kashmiris who were mulling a political career. Some of my friends in Kashmir quickly joined this party. Kashmir's youth are keenly interested in politics but sadly none of the traditional parties would open their doors for them. Finally, some of my colleagues joined the regional parties. Wahududin Parra joined the PDP and Junaid Mattu, the National Conference. Mattu came from a political background; his great-grandfather was a contemporary of Sheikh Mohammad Abdullah. After completing his education in USA he joined Sajjad Lone as spokesperson of his party—Peoples' Conference.

I was yet to make up my mind about the political party that I wanted to join.

I consulted some of my friends. Sajjad asked me to rejoin his party. However, he admitted that due to lack of resources, he had no plans of expanding the operations of Peoples' Conference and would prefer to concentrate on Handwara and other constituencies of North Kashmir. Former Law minister Muzzafar Beg advised me against joining PDP as, he felt, I would not be allowed to grow there. Once a top-ranking leader of the PDP, Beg had fallen out with the father-daughter duo of the PDP—Mufti Mohammad Sayeed and Mehbooba Mufti. He had been sidelined and elevated as a member of the Rajya Sabha. Interestingly, becoming a member of Rajya Sabha is seen as a punishment and a sinecure in Kashmir and therefore not liked by active politicians. Beg too was left with almost no role in the state or the party. Everyone told me that youngsters with no political backing and background had no future in Kashmir-based political parties that continue to treat the 70-year-olds as 'youth leaders'.

I left for Delhi where I discussed my plans to join a political party with my BJP contacts. Ravi Shankar Prasad quickly invited me to join the BJP. Prasad told me that he would arrange for my formal joining in Delhi in the presence of BJP chief Rajnath Singh. I was informed that I should keep myself free for a tentative date for the function. I was excited and waited for a call from Delhi. One day the phone rang; the caller at the other end introduced himself as an official from the office of Chief Minister of Gujarat Narendra Modi. Modi had just been nominated as the Prime Ministerial candidate of the BJP for 2014 elections. He informed me that Modiji wanted me to join the party at a rally in Hiranagar, Jammu, after a few days. This was unbelievable. How life changes! Here I was not even welcome in the state parties and now the man who could become the Prime Minister of India soon was going to welcome me into his party.

It was Modi's first campaign rally for 2014 general elections after being named as a PM nominee. It turned out to be the most memorable day of my life. I could see a sea of humanity in front of the dais where Modi was to speak. Modiji introduced me as his younger brother; he hugged me while announcing my entry into BJP. He praised me profusely. He said I had made a name for myself in journalism and it was time for me to work for the nation. I was so emotional. I remember kissing Modiji in full public view. It was a typical Kashmiri reaction and way of greeting. I was overwhelmed.

The news about my joining the BJP appeared in all the Delhi-based newspapers and the event was captured live by all television channels. I was asked to work with the Jammu office for my apprenticeship. I had to learn and understand how a national political party works. I stayed in Jammu for ten days. Even though I had no political mandate, nor did I hold any position, yet the Jammu colleagues treated me as one of their own; everyone helped me inside the office and outside too. Ashok Koul, an RSS leader from Kashmir, in particular, treated me as a student. He taught me many small and big things that are part of political life, the etiquettes of a politician and also educated me about the who's who of the party. Besides, he made me feel very comfortable inside the party office. With Koul sahib around

I never felt I was a political orphan. I became the first Kashmiri Muslim to be appointed as BJP spokesperson for Kashmir.

I was given ample freedom to play my two-year innings as party spokesperson for Kashmir.

In 2015, BJP and PDP entered into an alliance to rule J&K. It was the most unlikely political scenario as no party had a clear mandate. The people had given a divided verdict. Interestingly, BJP had won from Jammu and PDP from Kashmir after the two had campaigned as ideological rivals. However, perhaps due to the foresight and sense of responsibility of their leaders, the two parties could cobble a coalition government with clear terms of mutual engagement.

In the new dispensation, I was appointed vice-chairperson of the Jammu and Kashmir Projects Construction Corporation (JKPCC); it came with the ex-office status of Minister of State. JKPCC is a PSU under the state government and it undertakes construction of infrastructure projects. In its 62-year existence, the Corporation has never been headed by a politician.

My elevation was not just a job for me; it signalled a major change in the way politics is seen in Kashmir. It gave a clear signal to young people that one does not have to be a son, a daughter or a relative of a leader to be given a good position and trusted with responsibilities. People in Kashmir had become cynical; nobody trusted the system's propensity for treating people on merit. When I took over as vice chairman of the JKPCC, it trashed this perception. I was a common Kashmiri with no political backing. People would say behind my back, "*Dekho, BJP ne Khalid ko kaise accommodate kiya.* (See how BJP has accommodated Khalid)."

The day I took charge of the office, I made it clear to my staff that everyone was to be treated on merit; nobody should be discriminated against or favoured because of his links with parties or political past. No wonder, my office received visitors from families of separatists.

Inside the corporation, the work culture was poor. The officers and staff were given to believe that the corporation was supposed to help the kith and kin of the top leaders and bureaucrats, who comprised the Kashmiri elite. Many projects worth crores were allocated even without floating tenders. This organisation was part of a well-oiled machinery in Kashmir that was used to make the rich richer and the poor more deprived. Contracts for job works were often allocated to kitchen friends of the elite. I unearthed nearly 120 cases of irregularities wherein rules and procedures were bypassed to favour certain people.

This organised loot of resources by an oligarchy was the key reason for the gun to arrive in Kashmir; leaders were misusing democracy and its fruits were not reaching the common people. The center had been funding the State rather generously. However, there was no accountability of the money's usage. I soon realised that most of the people in positions had either a personal or a political interest in pushing files and spending on developmental works. Leaders of all parties used funds to create their own pocket boroughs of support and thus divided people; they could never think of the collective good of Kashmir. This is the reason behind the rampant cynicism about politics and intense hate for politicians in Kashmir.

Interestingly, in the initial days, I had to work from the outhouse of a government building that housed the office of JKPCC. Not because there was no space for me, but the people were so entrenched in the system that they saw my presence as an intrusion in their cozy world where bureaucrats and politicians shared the spoils of the system. Thc Managing Director was apparently under directions of political bosses. He was asked to block my entry into the office and to please his masters he tried to bully me. Every day, I would inquire about my office space and his standard reply would be that he was busy and would speak to me later. On the phone, his staff would tell me that the boss was in a meeting either with the Chief Minister or Governor. One day, I finally ran out of patience and gave him a tongue lashing. The officer was a gentleman and he started panicking. He later admitted to me that he was following orders from the top. Finally, PWD minister Nayeem Akhtar and Deputy Chief Minister Nirmal Singh intervened and made sure I got my office space and a chair.

In Kashmir, the chief minister and bureaucrats are generally locked in a cozy relationship. For this reason, the bureaucrats never bother to be responsive to the public as they feel secure in cultivating the top bosses and are, therefore, least bothered about the backlash of their indifference to the real problems of the common man.

My wife Susan was apprehensive on my joining the BJP as she felt it would bring the family in the public eye. She felt I was taking risks beyond my capacity. Susan told me that only the rich and the influential Kashmiris could go for bold choices as they could easily escape to their safe homes in Delhi and Jammu at the slightest hint of danger to their lives. She said that in Kashmir politics was for the privileged Muftis and Omar

Abdullahs and not for simple and straightforward people like me. Her concerns about our family's safety and privacy were genuine.

Holding the national flag in Kashmir comes at a cost. However, someone would have to do that duty. It was indeed a challenge that I accepted with all humility and sincerity.

After I was appointed as spokesperson of BJP, I witnessed bizarre reactions from politicians. Leaders of the mainstream parties called me. I felt most of them simply wanted to instill fear in me. They asked me to be careful since terrorists and their supporters could burn down my house and harm my family. It may sound unbelievable today, the fact is that the same advice and reassuring remarks also came from the separatists' camp. In fact, many pro-Pakistan leaders congratulated me for my baptism in politics.

Many people called me on behalf of the senior Hurriyat leaders to compliment and appreciate my bold stand of going with the BJP. One of them told me that there was a desperate need for a new leadership and new ideas to change the narrative. Another person said the separatists were tired and had realised that the gun would not solve the problem. Many Kashmiris told me that they believed the issue of Kashmir could be resolved only during the tenure of Narendra Modi.

I am happy at my association with the BJP; happier to see the admiration my family and neighbours have for me. They see me as a political activist and nothing else. In fact, the turmoil one sees in Kashmir is because of peoples' anger with regional parties. Each regional party comes with a new slogan—like PDP for self-rule and National Conference for political autonomy, thereby perpetuating the collective victimhood of the society.

However, one must pay tribute to the wisdom of the common Kashmiri. He is not communal; he understands the truth even though many a time he may not be in a position to take a stand due to multiple pressures.

Grooming In Politics

Seen from Kashmir, BJP and the other pro-Hindu groups looked like monsters out to eliminate Muslims. I too grew up imbibing the same impressions. Though due to my foray into activism, I was more aware of Indian politics, yet, strangely, I realised I was as nervous as a bride while entering the BJP office in Jammu for the first time.

The party office in Jammu is housed in an old building named after Pandit Ghirdhari Lal Dogra, a tall leader of Jan Sangh. The view from across the Peerpanjal, however, is that Dogra was responsible for launching an agitation against the then popular leader Sheikh Mohammad Abdullah in 1953, after Jan Sangh stalwart Shyama Prasad Mukherjee had died mysteriously in police lockup in Kathua. Mukherjee had defied the law and entered Jammu without obtaining the requisite permit. He was protesting against the mandatory permit that the non-state subjects or the outsiders were required to obtain before crossing into the state. He was arrested and put in the lockup in Kathua police station where he died the same night. Mukherjee was a visionary as he could foresee that the special status of Jammu and Kashmir would, one day, come in the way of the State's integration with India. In fact, he had coined the slogan *ek nishan, ek vidhan, ek pradhan* (One flag, one Constitution, and one leader) to emphasise on the basics of a nation's unity. He waged a battle for ending the ambiguous status of the state in the Union of India.

The version of history that most people in Kashmir believed is that Dogra was a 'Dogra' chauvinist and, therefore, anti-Muslim. Though the Jan Sangh's agitation had nothing to do with the dismissal of the Abdullah government in August 1953 and Sheikh's arrest, the furor over Mukherjee's death seemed to have added to his deteriorating relationship with New Delhi.

At a first look, the building didn't look impressive. The inside was no better. The party office had no parking space. I was nervous as I thought I may be the first Kashmiri Muslim to enter the premises in the capacity of a party member. I must have looked like a sacrificial lamb. I was shivering; the fear about the monster living behind Peerpanjal was apparently playing out inside my mind despite my bravado.

I joined the BJP on March 24, 2014. At that time, Jammu was already reeling under the summer heat while in Kashmir the spring blossoms were metamorphosing the landscape. In fact, the day I walked into the party office nobody was aware of my joining. I had recently met Jugal Kishore, BJP President, and, therefore, he was the only one who knew about my joining. My fears started subsiding as I was welcomed with a traditional ritual—distribution of *ladoos*. I was showered with genuine warmth by my party colleagues.

As I walked in, everyone I passed by offered me a *namaskar*. I was ushered into a small office where a white, kurta-clad man in his late sixties greeted me, "Khalidji, *namaskar*." He introduced himself as Ashok Koul, General Secretary of the Party. Koul sahib had served as the Principal of the Vishwa Bharati School, the only community school of the Kashmiri Pandits in the Valley. He was an RSS man and had recently been shifted to BJP.

Koul sahib's business-like yet warm attitude towards me was reassuring. He appreciated my decision to join BJP and told me this would be very good for me. After exchanging pleasantries, he gave me a booklet containing contact numbers of all officer bearers and a diary for jotting down notes. Soon Sat Sharma, a chartered accountant and party leader, joined us in the room. I also saw others like Bali Bhagat, Jugal Kishore, Chander Prakash Ganga, who later became ministers. They all entered Koul's chamber and crowded it. Though people were courteous, I had a feeling that some of them were uncomfortable with my presence in the office. Koul sahib must have realised this; he suddenly told me I could leave for the day and he would call me at an appropriate time. As I was leaving, some of the Kashmiri pandit members of the party lustily greeted me and demanded I throw a party to celebrate my joining. We all went to the Dak Bungalow on Residency Road and relished a Wazwan meal. Over the meal, I collected valuable tips on the lobbies inside the party. I was briefed about people who drink and those who eat non-vegetarian food. This knowledge proved useful as many of my colleagues are shy of admitting their eating preferences in public. Theirs turned out to be the most honest assessment of personalities and their respective roles in the party and this helped me get connected to everyone in the party. They also briefed me about the undeclared jurisdictions of various leaders.

At the end of the luncheon meeting, I was happy to have received a proper feedback from my friends. My exposure to international diplomacy at the United Nations and other international conferences had helped me understand the matrix of BJP rather quickly.

However, during the course of my work with the party over the next few months, a strange thought struck my mind—my party looked more like a trade union where everyone was angry. Leaders and workers hardly behaved as members of a ruling party; most would react to situations with anger and threats. Within three months of my joining the party, I was appointed the spokesperson for Kashmir region. It was a major responsibility and honestly, I felt I was not qualified for it. However, my bosses in the party told me all I had to do was to work freely without any apprehensions. The only instruction I got was that I should always work for the national interest and in favour of the party while taking positions on key matters in front of the media.

Being a spokesperson of a political party in the era of Television debates and live telecasts is an unenviable position; to take a position on each burning issue of Kashmir was the most challenging task. In my heart, I realised it was great on the part of my leaders to have entrusted me this responsibility. When I went to take a brief from the leaders they told me that since I knew Kashmir quite well I should speak without fear. There has been no occasion when my party instructed me to take a particular position or questioned my stand before the media.

As spokesperson of a national party I learnt how to work under pressure and deal with pessimists who were swarming all around. This role made me a public figure. My party was apparently happy with my performance and probably for this I was made the Vice Chairman of the J&K Projects Construction Corporation (JKPCC), a PSU under the state government.

In the fall of 2017, I visited the United States of America as a fellow of the South East Asia Center for Peace Studies. The Center is a government supported think tank based in Pennsylvania. Those three months were eventful for me. I was invited by the Indian Embassy to Washington, DC, to speak at the Deen Dayal Upadhaya centenary at the Capitol Hill. Ram Madhav gave me opportunity to speak. The hall was jam-packed with Indians. I was supposed to speak on Integral Humanism. The audience applauded my speech many times. I spoke from the heart. I told them about the aspirations and deprivations of the youth of Kashmir. I told them how many young Kashmiris were yearning to be part of the BJP and other national parties; they were sick of the cult of violence. I was overwhelmed at the generous applause I received from the Indian diaspora. It was a proud moment for me. Here I was, a Kashmiri Muslim, speaking on key national issues before an international audience. Foreign reporters covering the event showed keen interest in me.

That day I realised the real meaning of Koul sahib calling my decision to join BJP as a 'good' one. My party has given me enough headroom for expressing myself freely; it has never imposed any narrative on me. I realised that in BJP a political activist is trained and not tutored to be a leader. Leaders rise organically and they are not transplanted, as it happens in other political parties. I have always been told to take a stand for my people.

The US trip was a turning point for me; I felt stronger to speak in public. I was no longer a reluctant public speaker.

I worked on understanding the BJP as a political party. Since our state headquarter was in Jammu, I bought a flat in the winter capital within six months as I was visiting the party office at least thrice a month. I found that many BJP leaders and activists indeed had deep prejudices against Kashmiris. I had several meetings with individual leaders usually over a meal explaining to them things about Kashmir and trying to dispel the myths they nurtured in their minds against Kashmiris, especially Muslims. I worked hard to make myself relevant to the party. I made most of my colleagues realise that Kashmiri Muslims are nationalists and they can associate with BJP. I also made them realise that many a time the party ends up abusing Kashmiri Muslims in its press releases and that was not helping the party in making inroads into the Valley.

I would have regular meetings with Ashok Koul as part of my learning process. Initially, I would also meet members who would speak openly about their self-assigned mission to 'teach' Kashmiris (Muslims) a lesson. They had a firm belief that all Muslims in Kashmir were with Pakistan. With my presence and interaction with them, such talk was no longer heard openly. Koul sahib became my teacher and a close friend. Within a few months, the party gave me a free hand to speak on their behalf. By this time, I was friends with many top leaders. I realised that most of them loved non-vegetarian food. They would often tell me stories of the connection between the Dogra people and the Kashmiris.

During the crucial 2014 general election, I was made in charge of the media cell. The cell was responsible for creating buzz about BJP in Kashmir even though the party was not a serious contender for votes in the Valley. We launched a media blitzkrieg. In fact, the media was a strategic team and we worked under the guidance of senior party leader Ram Madhav. During the run-up to the Assembly elections the same year, I organised a mega event—Vision Kashmir 2020—in the SKICC, where senior BJP leaders including the then Finance Minister Arun Jaitley interacted with business leaders, traders, and intellectuals of Kashmir. The idea of the conference was to communicate with people of Kashmir and to roll out the roadmap of development in Kashmir. Going by the turnout and the response of the audience, the conference was a huge success.

Our media cell was a success as we could hit the target of speaking to all the media persons in Kashmir. Out vote share in Kashmir had increased though we all knew it was too early for us to dream of winning an election from Kashmir.

When Prime Minister Narendra Modi took the oath of office in May 2014, I was among those privileged to be present. Thereafter, I was nominated as spokesperson of the BJP in Jammu and Kashmir. It was again a major responsibility as I would be required to speak to the media and attend live debates on anything related to Kashmir. Back in those days, Kashmir was swarming with media persons representing national and international publications, television channels and radios. In all my interviews, I advocated free and fair Assembly elections in Kashmir.

My friend and former colleague Sajjad Lone had met PM Modi before the elections. I have always admired his courage; this time, he could smell the coffee and foresee that BJP would win. By meeting Modi, Lone had cobbled a pre-poll alliance with the party. Sajjad would tell people in his election rallies about this meeting with Modi; he called Modiji his elder brother. The fact is, at the end of this, Sajjad was a winner. He won a handsome victory from Handwara. It was clear that his voters had not rejected him because he had sided with BJP or Mr Modi. His victory should have opened the eyes of all those who keep saying that Muslims are against BJP. Later, Sajjad became a minister in the PDP-BJP coalition government and was decidedly the best performing member of the cabinet. In fact, Sajjad was made a minister in the BJP quota. Sajjad's tryst with electoral politics in Kashmir is a lesson for all those who stereotype Kashmiris and see the people from the eyes of a few dynasties that have looted Kashmir and kept its people in perpetual confusion about the status of their state.

In his public discourses, Sajjad speaks about changing the lives of people through development; he never talks about *azadi*, Hindustan-Pakistan or *jihad* and yet he is a popular leader.

On the eve of counting of the votes, Ram Madhav and other colleagues visited my home for dinner. Susan had prepared a vegetarian meal and the dinner led to a very useful interaction with Madhavji. We all sat on the floor in typical Kashmiri style to have our food. Madhavji was relaxed; he spoke to us and each sentence was a learning for me. Personally, I never miss an opportunity to listen to Madhavji. For young BJP members, Ram Madhav is a modern RSS *pracharak*. Many other RSS leaders whom I have met are generally in the age group of sixty and above. Madhavji remains an iconic figure for the young BJP members.

That evening Madhavji was apparently happy at Sajjad Lone's work and he thought he would win the election. He said Sajjad's politics was the silver lining in Kashmir's complicated political scenario. He said even if BJP did not win a seat from Kashmir, we must celebrate Sajjad's impending victory.

Madhavji had also played a key role in cementing the coalition arrangement between PDP and BJP after the result was announced. In fact, to avoid the prying media, he and Haseeb Drabu of the PDP had shifted to Mumbai where they finalised the agenda of the alliance over several rounds of brainstorming.

PDP and BJP were, in fact, strange bedfellows to be getting into an alliance. The two had campaigned hard against each other; BJP had campaigned against Mehbooba Mufti's soft separatism and PDP leaders had warned Kashmiris about the Modi government's diabolic plans about them. In the Mumbai talks, the two sides acknowledged the differences and worked out a unique formula for giving the State a government and at the same time honouring the public mandate. The two parties divided their areas of responsibility; BJP to take care of Jammu with the PDP in charge of Kashmir. The arrangement worked till June 2018 when the BJP decided to pull out of the coalition.

It's hard for the leaders to see a Kashmiri Muslim joining BJP. I had ignored the disapproving talk of many but once when a senior National Conference leader tried to demoralise me publicly I gave it back to him. It happened at Jammu airport when I was returning from Delhi. NC legislator from Jammu, Devinder Singh Rana, tried to make light of my political affiliation. Pointing towards me he told a senior police officer in the presence of everyone, "Give him full security for a BJP worker in Kashmir is a rare species."

I didn't take this jibe kindly and retorted in the same vein, "Local parties better watch out as the national parties expand their wings in Kashmir. It will be hard for the regional parties to accept the fact of our presence in the Valley." I don't think Rana took it sportingly.

However, though we are working hard, I have realised that BJP can't grow in Kashmir till it is under Jammu office. There is a fundamental anomaly in BJP's approach to Kashmir. The party gets votes from Jammu by badmouthing Kashmiris. This leads to an awkward situation for people like me in Kashmir. However, I must say a new leadership of BJP with a better perspective and understanding of Kashmir is rising. These leaders are mostly in the age group of 20-40 years. I feel BJP as a political force is evolving in J&K and, gradually, it is opening up to new ideas and perspectives.

With my association with BJP, I have proven a point—Kashmiri Muslims are as nationalistic as anyone else.

Epilogue

A FRESH BEGINNING

After I joined BJP, people often approached me with problems and I was visiting the Civil Secretariat more often. It was the time when PDP and BJP had together formed the government. The secretariat buildings in Srinagar and Jammu could be rated as the most fortified offices in the country and getting in wasn't easy for me. Going through frisking and multiple security checks to enter, I wondered how difficult it was for ordinary people, especially Kashmiri youth, to get inside. Interestingly, I found hordes of young girls and boys waiting outside the offices of ministers and secretaries. It's another reality that most would return without meeting the officers.

When I would go past the waiting men and women to see the same officer or minister, I would find them engaged in no substantial work. They would be often planning their vacation in Dubai or London; some would be discussing the design options for their new house. The ministers would remain mostly inside their fortified and secured official bungalows without any connect whatsoever with the people outside. The public, especially the youth, seemed of no concern to them.

As I often interacted with the waiting men and women, I discovered most of them had come from far off places. They wanted the roads to their villages repaired, piped water supply and a majority wishing to get a government job.

As a representative of a party, I felt Prime Minister Narendra Modi and BJP's vision of a peaceful Kashmir and youth could fulfill their aspirations.

Delhi had shared this vision with the then Chief Minister Mehbooba Mufti, soon after she took charge of the PDP-BJP coalition government. In fact, she was told that Delhi wanted to see the young generation of Kashmir involved in nation building. To be fair to her, Mehbooba Mufti's government had its baptism by fire. Within three months, the government was faced with a serious law and order situation. On June 8, Army and Police had zeroed in on a hideout in a South Kashmir village and killed Burhan Wani, a young terrorist of Hizbul Mujahideen. Burhan, a school dropout, was more of a social media hero than a real hardcore terrorist. His death sparked off protests and South and Central Kashmir almost slipped into mayhem and chaos that lasted for four months. The security honchos didn't anticipate such a groundswell of anger at what they thought was a routine killing of an ordinary terrorist. The police had to deal with armies of violent youth in streets, fields and highways. The ubiquitous stone as a deadly missile in the hands of young protesters gave the forces a tough time. The mob terrorised common people as well and the vigilante groups imposed a near complete ban on movement of traffic inside Srinagar and on the highway. In South Kashmir, these groups attacked police stations, beat up the cops and took away weapons from the armoury. At a couple of places, policemen were lynched.

Amidst this, a worried Prime Minister called Mehbooba Mufti to Delhi for a serious discussion. He told her clearly that she should go for panchayat and local body elections immediately. In fact, the last local body election in the State was held in 2005 and Panchayat election in 2011. Delhi believed that elected representatives of 4,490 Panchayat bodies and other Municipal bodies would infuse optimism in the situation and bring about a significant change on the ground, especially in the Valley. Deep in their hearts, BJP leaders had realised that Kashmir needs grass roots democracy that can give stakes to people in governance. Let me admit (and I am privy to many things to conclude this), it was also an indirect way of propping up a new leadership against two families—Abdullahs and the Muftis—who took turns to rule the State, albeit through a democratic exercise.

Mehbooba had apparently agreed. However, she changed her mind after holding consultations with her colleagues in Srinagar. Her party leaders told her that it was "*Dilli kee chaal*" (a common Kashmiri expression for Delhi's diabolic game plan and conspiracy theory). Delhi, they said, wanted to snatch away the powers of legislators and political leaders and pass these on to the Municipal councillors and elected village heads. Mehbooba was so influenced by these arguments that she chose to meet and discuss this with her arch rival Farooq Abdullah, leader of the National Conference. He also cautioned her against "*Dilli kee chaal*". The effervescent Farooq Abdullah openly threatened "Dilli" on its "*chaal*". Mehbooba dithered and backed out on her promise. She told Delhi that holding these elections would lead to increased violence in Kashmir.

I was told that this was the main reason for BJP to call off its alliance with PDP.

In fact, in Kashmir, all the political players rallied around PDP to thwart the civic and panchayat elections. The leaders were in no mood to share the power with ordinary men and women who mostly get elected to village panchayats.

On the other hand, Prime Minister Modi was keen to create stakes for the people in governance in J&K; he firmly believed this was needed to change the lingering discontentment and political hegemony of a couple of family-led parties. Elections were to be held at any cost. Surprisingly, the man in charge, Governor N N Vohra, didn't have conviction in this theory. Probably he had stayed on in Raj Bhawans in Jammu and Srinagar for too long—ten years—and was under the influence of politicians. Or, maybe Vohra was afflicted with the Stockholm Syndrome and, therefore, was not ready to look at an out of the box solution. He also told central leaders that holding local body and panchayat elections was not in the interests of the State!

Delhi was in no mood to listen to this; a new Governor Satya Pal Malik trooped into Srinagar's Raj Bhawan. For him, holding elections was at the top of his priority list.

To be fair to all, Kashmiri leaders and Modi government continued to hold discussions on panchayat elections. Delhi was keen that all political parties participate in the elections and, therefore, kept prodding leaders of PDP and NC. However, both the parties were adamant and kept saying terrorists would target their workers and voters and Kashmir would see massive violence. To delay the elections, the leaders asked Governor Malik to call an all-party meet. By now, Delhi had decided to go ahead with elections and dismissed their fears. Sensing the mood in Delhi, these leaders placed a fresh demand: the elections should be help on non-party basis. By then, Delhi was fed up of these haughty Kashmiri leaders and unhesitatingly said a big 'No' to their newest demand. Both National Conference and PDP had enjoyed power for years and when it was the turn of the common man in a village to get a share in governance, these leaders wanted to scuttle it.

Finally, Delhi called off the talks prompting Abdullah and the Mufti led political parties to announce they would boycott the election. The boycott was a sham. Both the parties linked their boycott to a Public Interest Litigation that questioned the status of Article 35A of the Constitution in the Supreme Court. Strange logic: is it the job of political parties to decide the nature of cases the apex court should hear?

I know that Abdullah and Mehbooba were sure that the Modi government would take their boycott seriously and would rush to Srinagar to pander to their whims. Kashmiri leaders had tried such blackmails in the past quite successfully. This time, it proved to be a miscalculation. They had no idea that they would be dealing with a regime with a different approach on Kashmir. The BJP government was ready to see democracy flourish in J&K even if it meant keeping two key political parties—NC and PDP—out of its ambit.

The rush of youth for party tickets to contest elections in fact unnerved the leadership of NC and PDP. They made a quiet U turn on their stand on elections and fielded their proxy candidates for each and every seat.

In the meanwhile, Junaid Mattu, who was well known for his television appearances as NC spokesperson, was upset with his party's decision. He met his former colleague Sajjad Lone and wished to quit his party. Next, we learnt that Junaid was a candidate for Srinagar Municipal Corporation and Lone and BJP had decided to extend their support to him. We, in the BJP, were excited to hear this. I remember Sajjad called Ram Madhav to tell him about Junaid. Madhavji flew to Srinagar for a closed-door meeting with Mattu and several other aspiring candidates.

A bit about my mentor and guru Ram Madhav: He remains the most accessible BJP leader for Kashmiris, especially youngsters. His outreach to the youth had increased manifold in the aftermath of Burhan Wani episode. Post Burhan Wani killing, security agencies were aghast at the intelligence inputs about large scale recruitment of local youth in terrorist organizations, especially Hizbul Mujahideen. Sadly, after Wani's killing, every young man wanted to pick up the gun. There were alarming reports about the presence of about 2,000 armed militants across the Line of Control, waiting to infiltrate into Kashmir. Young locals itching to join terrorists' ranks and the feared influx would make a deadly cocktail of violence.

Ram Madhav had a formula up his sleeve to address this scenario. It was that more young men and women should assume political roles. Giving them ownership of their land and affairs would end the romantic notion of gun, *jihad* and martyrdom. His calculation was that against 2,000 militants, the local urban body and panchayat elections would give the State, 5,500 Kashmiris in leadership roles. Today, this idea has become a reality in Kashmir.

Ram Madhav was passionate about empowering youth through elections. He made several low profile visits to Kashmir during this period and must have met at least 2,000 youth personally. His interactions with local youth were not publicised and care was taken to protect the identities of participants. I was present in most of the meetings. His message would be: neither Congress nor BJP would be able to deliver you *azadi*; whatever you get you will get from New Delhi. He also told them that the sky was the limit for Delhi when it came to 'giving' to its people in Kashmir. His interactions generated hope among the participants as they could see a way out of the quagmire that they found themselves in, in Kashmir.

Sajjad Lone's party, Peoples' Conference, fielded candidates from Srinagar and Kupwara for Municipal elections. In fact, he became the king maker in the election of a Mayor for Srinagar. In Ganderbal, we had founded an organization—All Jammu and Kashmir Youth Alliance—a year ago. Our members had been working on the ground mainly imparting leadership skills to the local youth. We fielded our candidates in the town and won 6 out of 18 seats.

The victory of Youth Alliance candidates in the Ganderbal Municipal Corporation was an exhilarating yet humbling experience. We celebrated our victory by paying obeisance at the shrine of Qamar sahib and distributing yellow rice among people. The enthusiasm of the newly elected counsellors had to be seen to be believed. I am sure these youngsters will work hard and grow in confidence to contest Assembly elections in due course.

For most of us, this election is the beginning of the end of plutocracy—the rule of a few families—the Muftis and the Abdullahs. This election is also a baby step towards the goal of making mainstream politics a viable career option for the youth.

During campaigning, I realised how common people—especially seasoned citizens—were realising they had been held hostage through crafted false narratives and slogans by a few families. Their slogans instigated people at an emotional level; the aim of the leaders was to perpetuate their rule by blackmailing Delhi with their indispensability. I have always wondered if the greater autonomy slogan of the National Conference was so popular, why did the party split in 1984? Why did, for that matter, Junaid Mattu leave the NC? Also, if the self rule (of the PDP) is a popular idea, why did Hamid Karra (a former MP) leave the party? People of all generations appreciated our guts and new way of thinking. During campaigning, we saw elders cheering our young candidates. That generation was happy to see a new crop of leaders coming up in their own small way.

Ganderbal has never fallen prey to the wave of terrorism. I can proudly say that people there are overtly pro-India. It happens to be the youngest of the districts, carved out in 2016. Though it has been a high profile constituency as both Farooq Abdullah and his son Omar Abdullah had chosen to contest their elections from here, it remains one of the most neglected areas. While North and South Kashmir have political patronage, Central Kashmir basked under the glory of being NC's bastion and never demanded any development. The Youth Alliance wants to play a positive role and that is the reason despite being the single largest group, it lent support to the new Mayor, an independent candidate. We want Ganderbal to become a major tourist attraction and have an AIIMS like institution. Ganderbal is water rich and we would press for power projects coming up on its rivers for the benefit of the district.

When I travel and meet people, I am often asked why the youth of Kashmir are angry and pelt stones at security forces. In fact, Pakistan or religious indoctrination is not the only reason for the youth to be up in arms. It's bizarre to see young boys, with no weapons and untrained in use of arms, defying security forces and even death. What is the reason behind this? One has to understand the deeper psychology behind this. For a young Kashmiri, security forces symbolise the power of Delhi, the federal government. Again, an average Kashmiri feels he has been wronged by corrupt Kashmiri leadership. He has a grudge against Delhi for supporting a corrupt oligarchy. He feels it's because of Delhi's support that Kashmiri leaders can dare to ignore the woes of common people. So, by fighting security forces, the youth are, in fact, venting their anger on New Delhi.

Kashmir's current generation is seething with resentment and they are proud to have learnt to fight back. Their message to New Delhi is loud and clear: we shall not budge before the nexus of corrupt leaders. They want New Delhi to investigate the scams that the corrupt have indulged in and looted the public money. Most of them have sent away their children to far off lands for education and work while they keep cheering the mourners as the coffins of young men are lowered in their graves rather prematurely. When Indian democracy has sent a charismatic and once tall national leader like Lalu Prasad Yadav to jail for corruption, a Kashmiri wonders why there is a different yardstick for Kashmir.

WHO FAILED KASHMIRIS?

Before the 2014 General Elections, there was a buzz about Gujarat model of development across the country. In fact, I was lucky to see its working on the ground. Narendra Modi was Chief Minister of Gujarat and the model was attributed to him. I had just joined the BJP when I got an invite to attend the Vibrant Gujarat Summit, a biannual business congregation where heads of companies from all over the world, investors, policy leaders etc. come under one roof to explore investment opportunities in Gujarat. In fact, Vibrant Gujarat was Modi's brainchild and since he was largely expected to win the coming Lok Sabha election, everyone seemed to be talking about it. I was lucky to attend the Vibrant Gujarat summit in 2013. The conference is organised at Mahatma Mandir, perhaps India's largest convention complex at Gandhi Nagar. For three days, business and trade leaders from all over the world converge at Mahatma Mandir and Gujarat government plays host. I attended the summit along with my business friends from Kashmir. In fact, the visit of a Kashmiri delegation to the Summit had attracted media coverage.

We returned with enthusiasm and optimism. Surely this model could be repeated in a State like ours, where natural and human resources are in plenty. "Vibrant Kashmir global

Summit," sounded a great idea. I was pleasantly surprised to see the idea gaining currency from across the political spectrum and sectors of economy. Even people with clear separatist leanings showed their support for Modi's development agenda. We managed to kindle hope in the hearts of people and revived their dream of economic development and general well being. Kashmir was seething with expectations about a huge round of development. Not many across India know this: people of Kashmir have a special bond with Gujarat. Even at the peak of terrorism, Gujarati tourists never stopped visiting Kashmir. A Gujarat based travel company remained in the forefront of reviving Kashmir's tourism industry when even locals had given it up in the face of rising terrorism and violence. This heartening gesture is remembered by people. So, when Gujarat resurfaced in the context of development, people were hoping the Gujarat-Kashmir link would forge greater bonds between businesses and trade between the two states. People in Kashmir conjured up images of an economic windfall through replication of Gujarat model.

We had decided to host Vibrant Kashmir Summit in Srinagar in September 2014. Some of my businessmen friends joined hands with me to make it a success. Everyone welcomed the idea. We were imagining big investors putting in money in projects and ventures in the State; Kashmiri businessmen being able to expand their business and young people getting plenty of jobs and livelihood opportunities.

Were we daydreaming?

We had sent the invitations to people across the country; Prime Minister Modi was supposed to inaugurate the summit.

Our enthusiasm was bursting at the seams when God disposed it off in one go. Kashmir was hit by unprecedented floods —the heaviest in living memory—Srinagar was nearly deluged. We had to announce postponement of the event and it never really took off. After the floods, Kashmir had Assembly elections.

MY CALLING

Just after the 2019 elections were announced, I was busy planning my trip to USA when I saw Ram Madhav's message on my mobile. : "Are you ready?" I wondered what I was to be ready for. "To contest elections," was his reply. Ram Madhav was sitting in the meeting of the BJP parliamentary board when he texted me. It was humbling to realise that my name was being discussed in the presence of Prime Minister Modi and BJP President Amit Shah.

My name as BJP candidate for Srinagar Lok Sabha constituency figured in the first list released by the party in Delhi. I was pitted against a stalwart like Farooq Abdullah, who is the son of the tallest of Kashmiri leaders, Sheikh Mohammad Abdullah. I knew my chances of winning the elections were bleak. I was contesting in a milieu where parties with whom BJP had alliances in the past were instrumental in fanning the idea that BJP was Kashmir's enemy. This was sheer hypocrisy since the leaders of NC and PDP were fine with BJP when it enabled them to be in power; now they were spreading rumours and hate against it when they were out of power.

As a candidate, countering this campaign was a huge challenge.

For elections, I shifted to Srinagar with my family and opened an election office.

I adopted a different style of campaigning. Instead of holding big election rallies, I would pay home visits and go for door-to-door campaigning in my hometown Ganderbal. I would visit families either early morning or evening to avoid focus on them. In fact, after Burhan Wani's death, no political party or leaders dared to put their banners on the roadside at public places. I am sure they feared these would be brought down in no time by angry people. I was the only contestant who had put up hoardings and billboards right from Kangan in North Kashmir to Budgam. My slogans for the electorate were *Khalid hai to Solid hai, Jhooth chhodo, Sach bolo*. The latter was a reference to the falsehood spread by regional parties among people.

Omar Abdullah took exception to my use of green backdrop for posters and other campaign material. I told him that green is part of our national flag and BJP does not distinguish between people on the basis of their religion. Later, Ram Madhav said BJP was not stuck with the idea of one colour. My candidature is not about winning or losing an election. I consider its outcome as a referendum for Kashmir's accession to India. If I fail, we need to question the parties that had aligned for power with New Delhi and have since distanced from it, about their fluctuating love for the country. While separatist leaders are ready to die for Pakistan, why do leaders and parties who got largesse from Delhi not even speak for India in Kashmir. In a way, their selfish and duplicitous stand is responsible for alienation in the Valley.

Ram Madhav used the election to carry on his outreach programme with the youth. At short notice, some 250 college students met him for an interaction. I was pleasantly surprised to see young men and women asking him tough questions. One asked why an accountability commission was not being set up in Kashmir to fix responsibility of politicians who are believed to have swindled public money. A young woman wanted Madhavji to ensure middlemen are removed from government deals.

The election taught me how to campaign gracefully. With this, I believe I have sown a seed of hope for the future. I will have to work hard for it to bloom and grow tall. At the end of a campaign, as I stand on the banks of the Sind and watch the sun rise and cast a golden hue on Qamar sahib's shrine, my heart fills with hope.

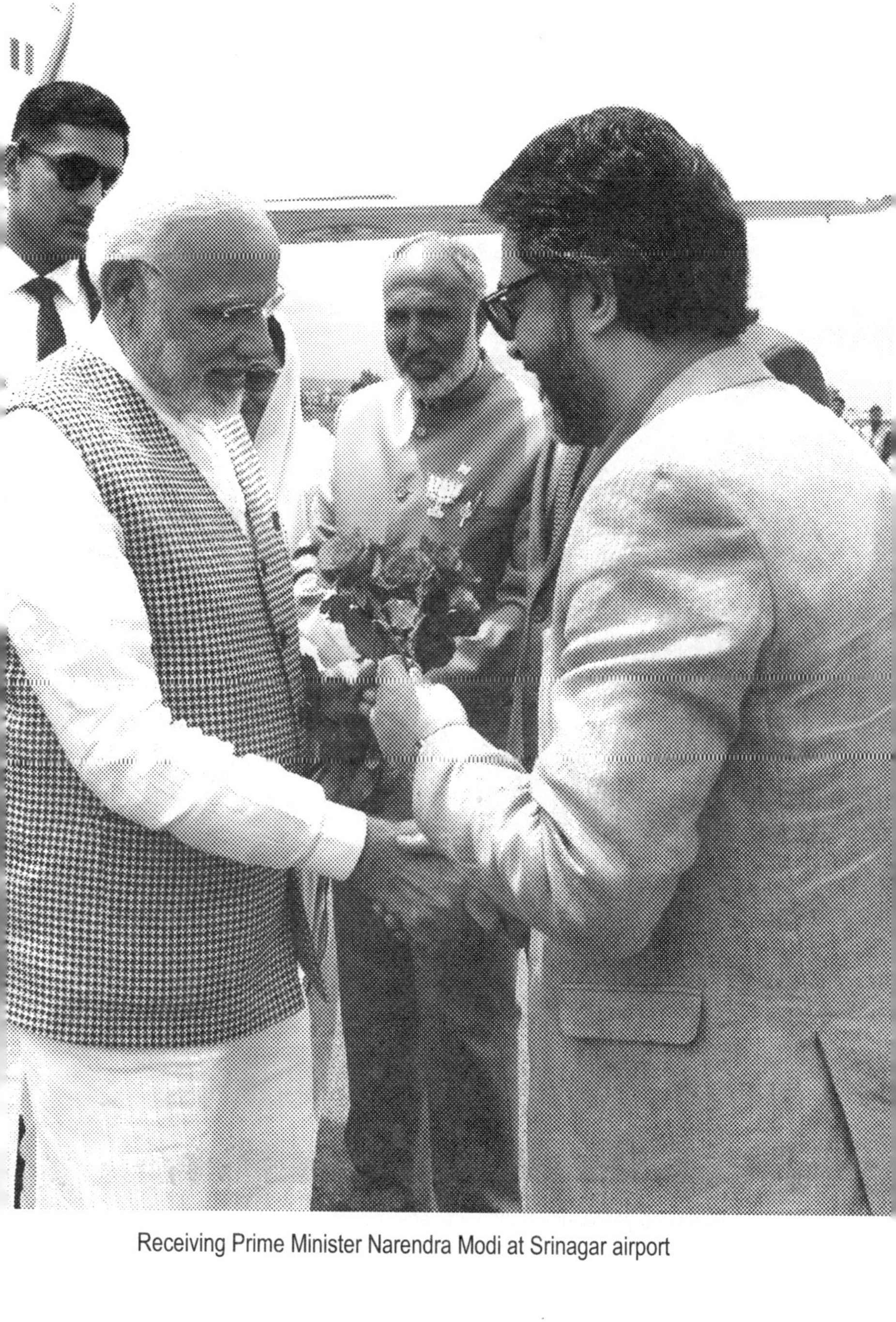

Receiving Prime Minister Narendra Modi at Srinagar airport

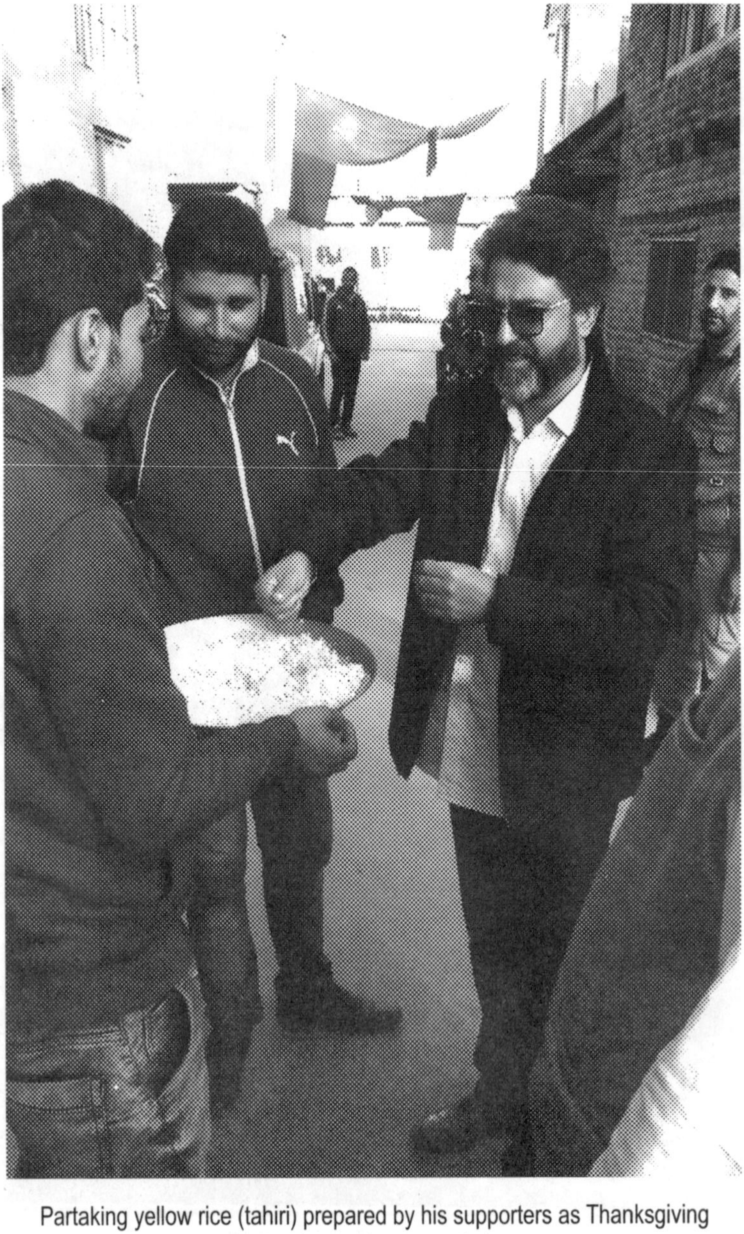

Partaking yellow rice (tahiri) prepared by his supporters as Thanksgiving for his election campaign

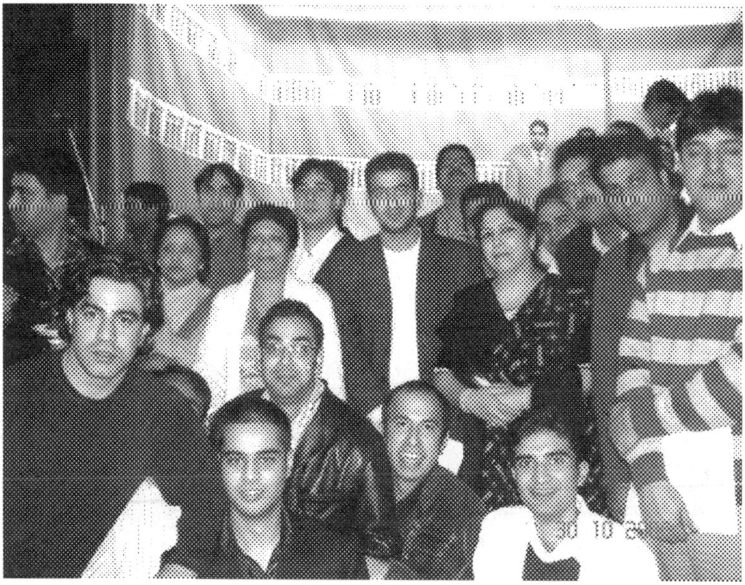

Burn Hall school alumni meet in Srinagar

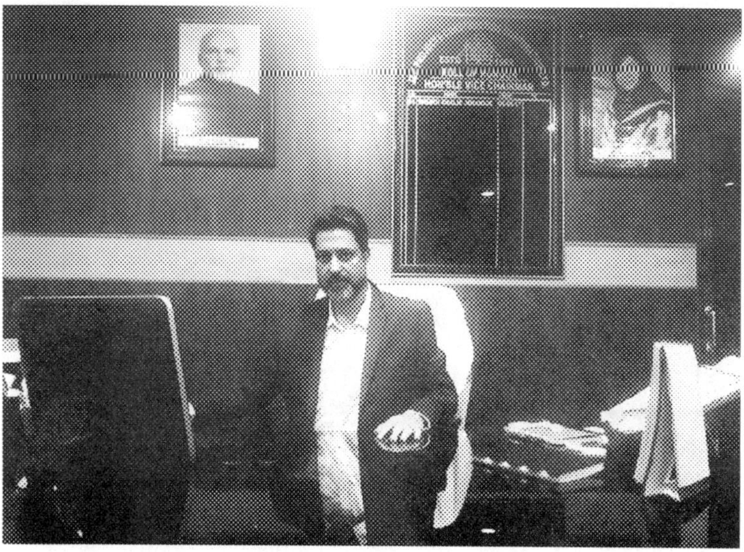

In his office of Chairman, JKPCC

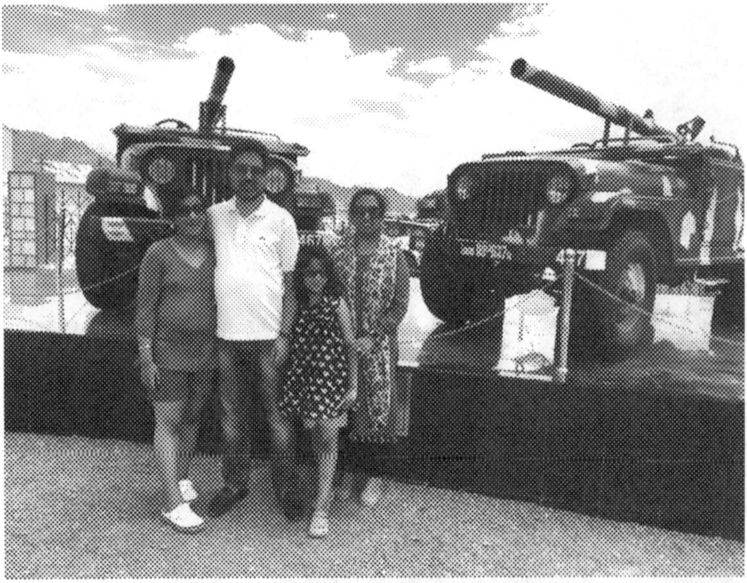

With wife Susan and daughters Sofia and Riana

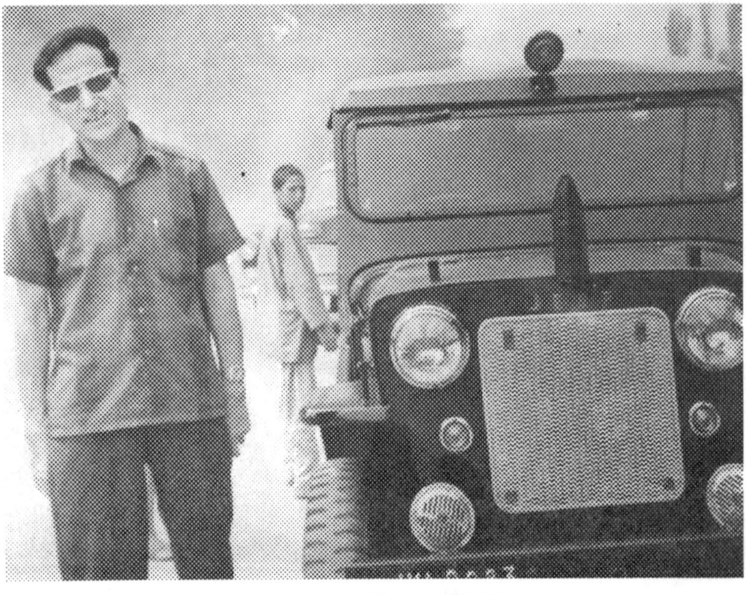

My father soon after the 1971 war

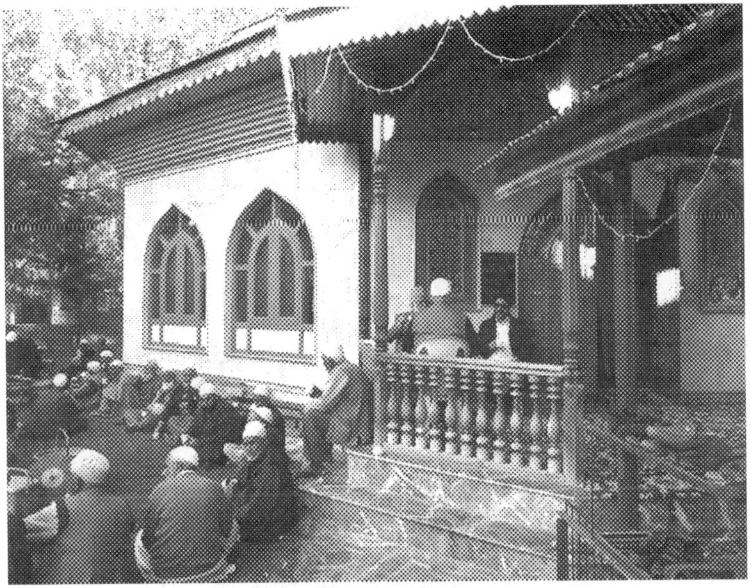

Celebrating the Urs of Qamar sahib

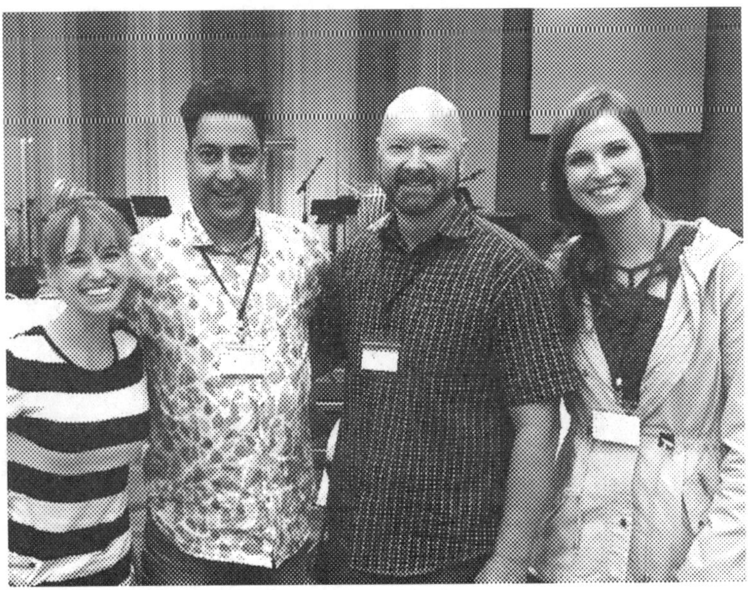

With colleagues during my fellowships in the USA

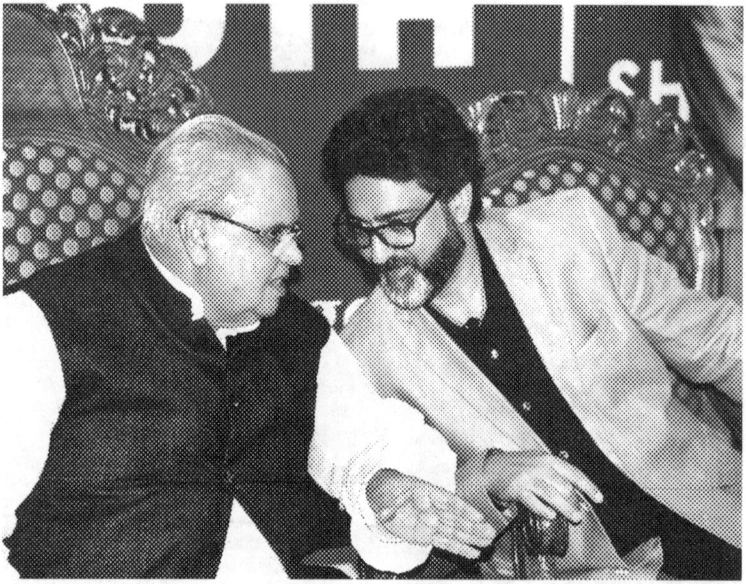

With Jammu and Kashmir Governor Satya Paul Malik

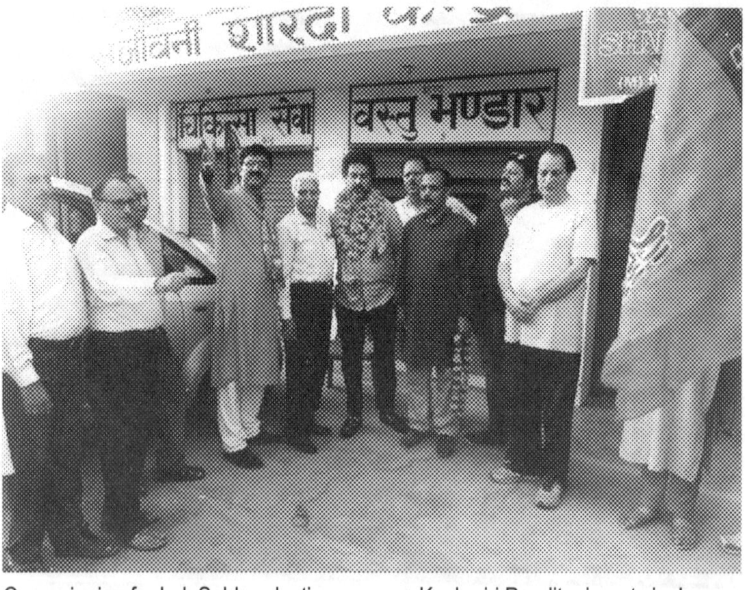

Campaigning for Lok Sabha elections among Kashmiri Pandit migrants in Jammu

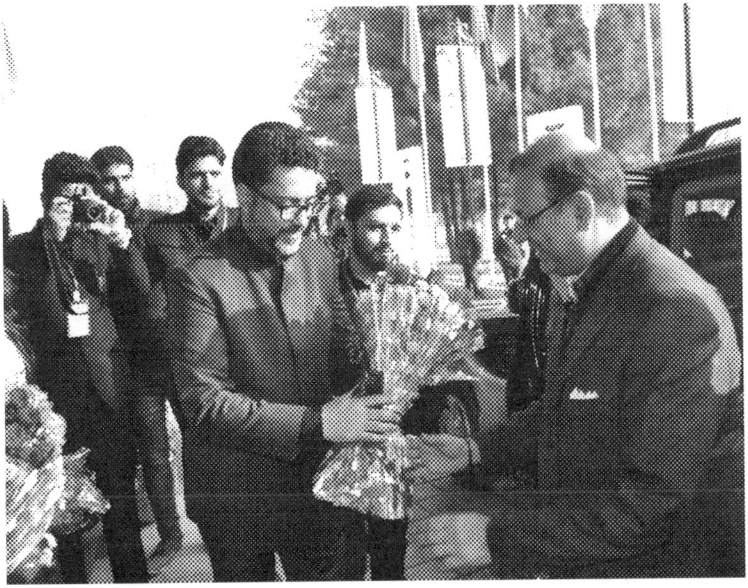

Receiving Member of Parliament Jayant Sinha for Ideas Conclave in Srinagar

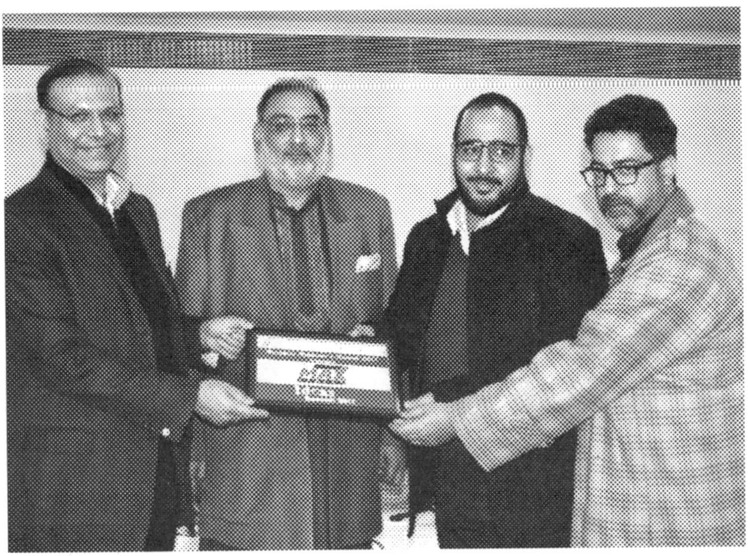

At the inauguration of Business and Political Weekly's Srinagar edition

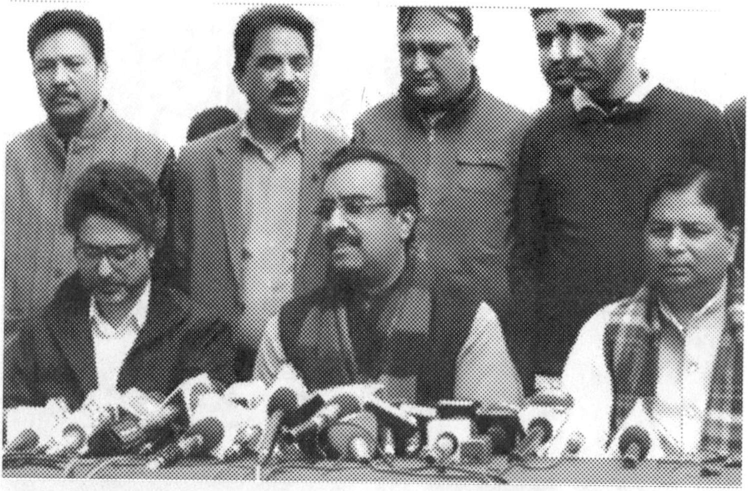

With my mentor and guru Ram Madhav in Srinagar during a press conference in Srinagar

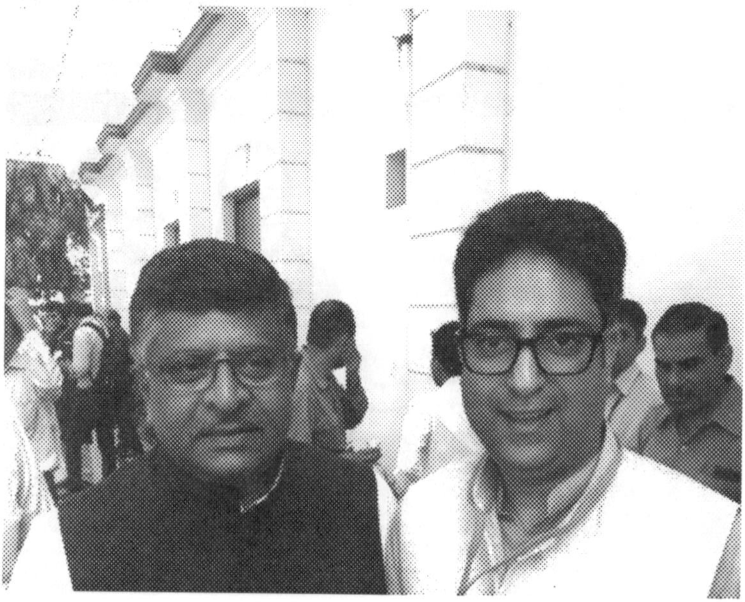

With BJPs Ravi Shankar Prasad

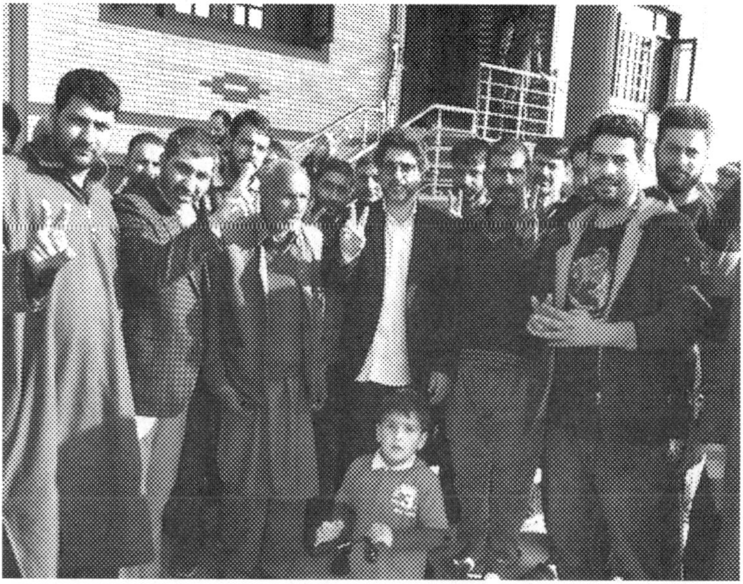

With supporters during election campaigning in Ganderbal

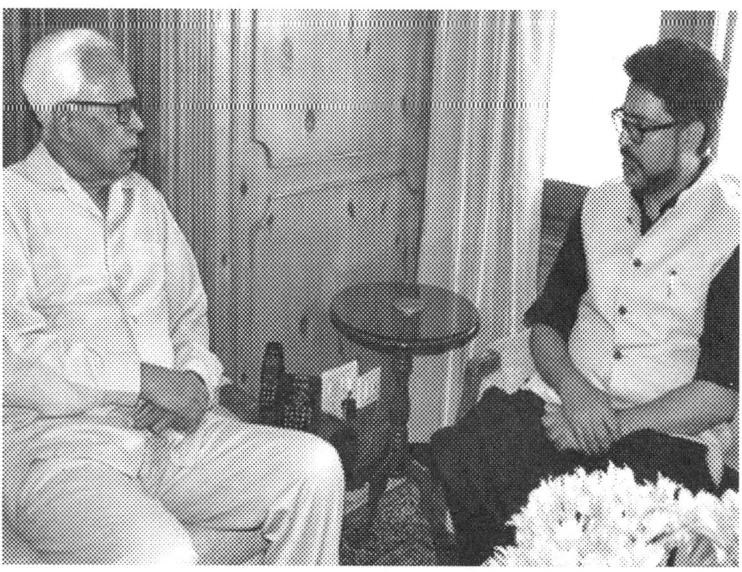

With former Governor N N Vohra

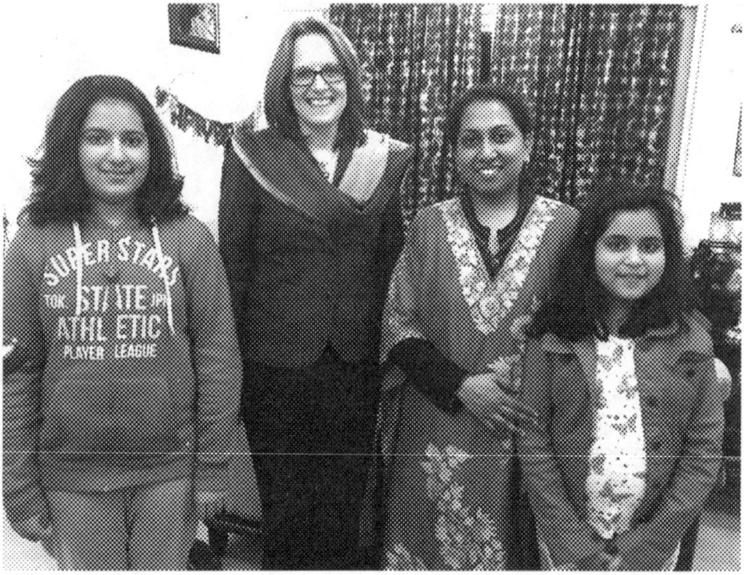

USA deputy NSA Lisa Curtis with Susan, Sofia and Rania at our home in Ganderbal

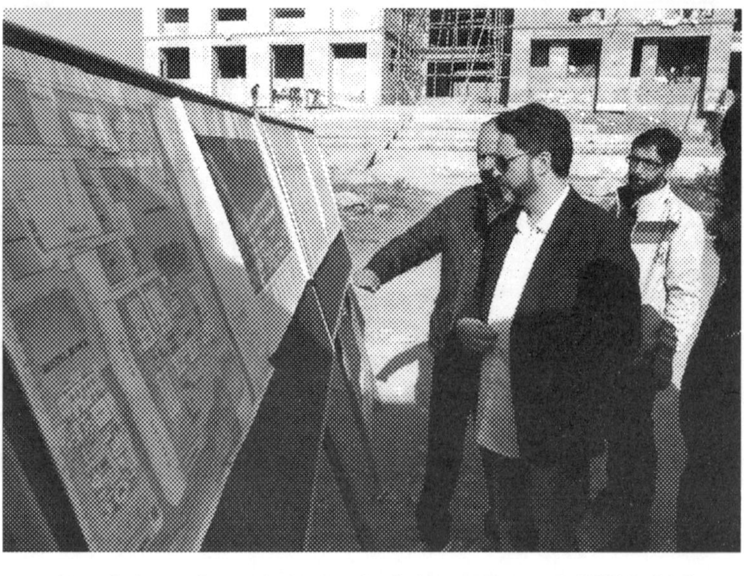

At work: Inspecting projects at a site during my tenure as JKPCC chief

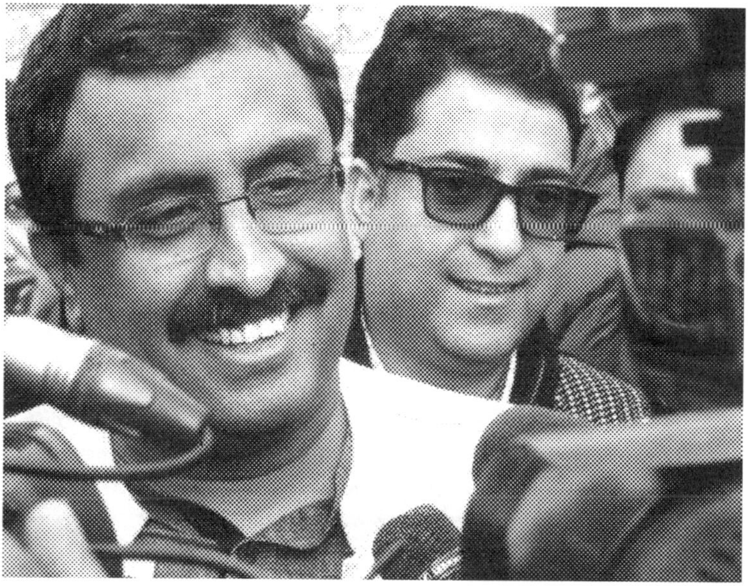

With Ram Madhav

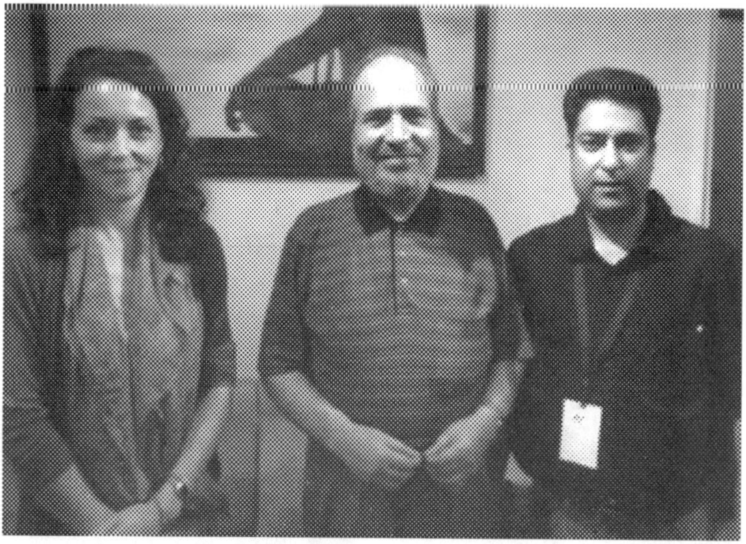

With former J&K minister Muzzafar Baigh

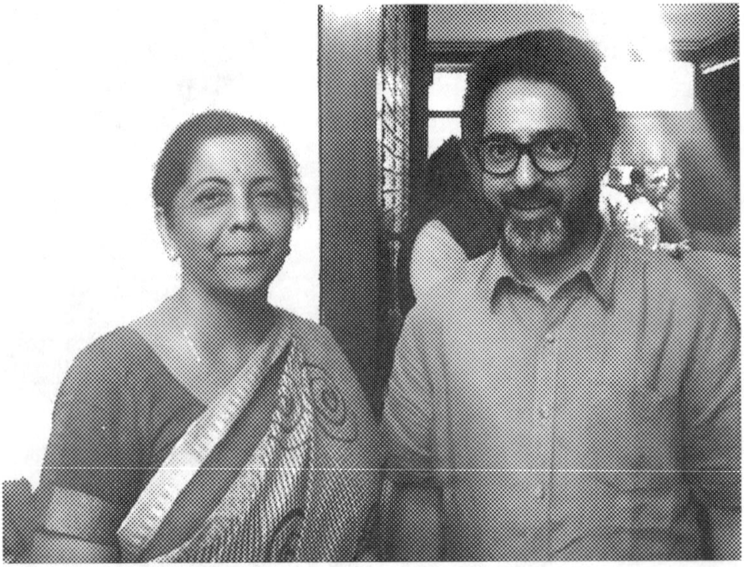

With Senior leader and Minister Nirmala Sitharaman

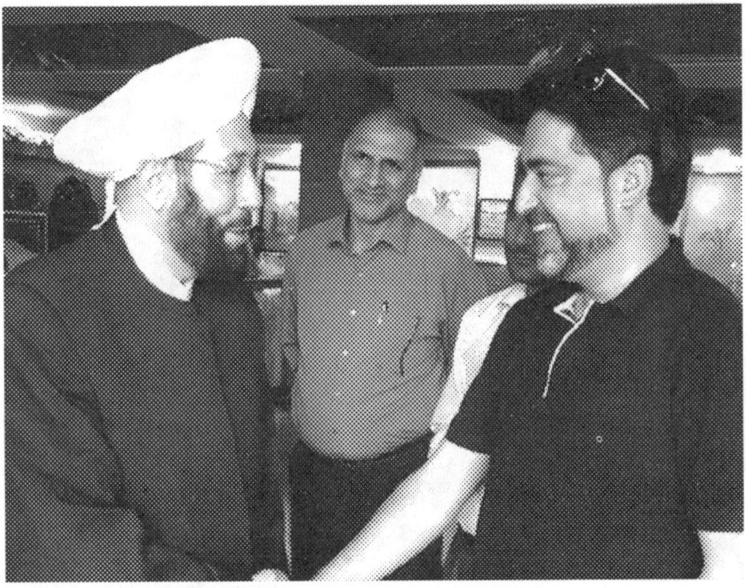

With an Imam in Syria during my visit as a journalist

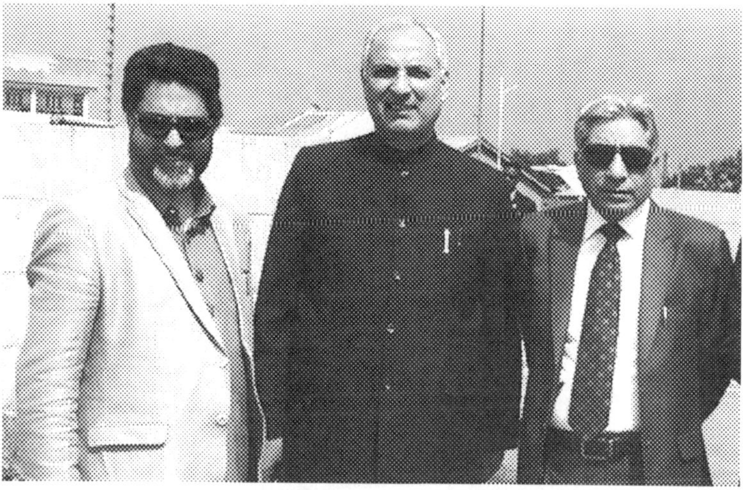

With PDP ministers Abdul Rehman Veeri and Ghulam Mohammad Hanjura in Srinagar

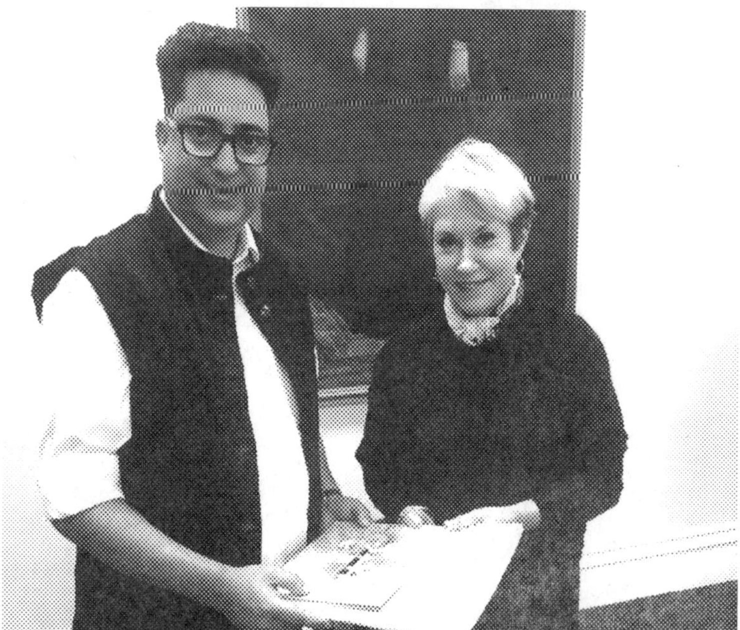

Receiving my fellowship at Peace and Conflict Institute at Washington, DC

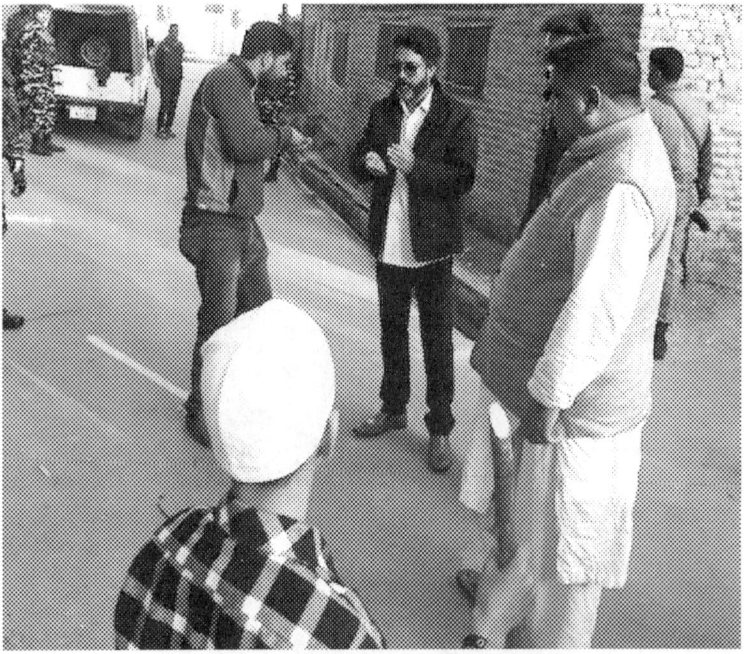

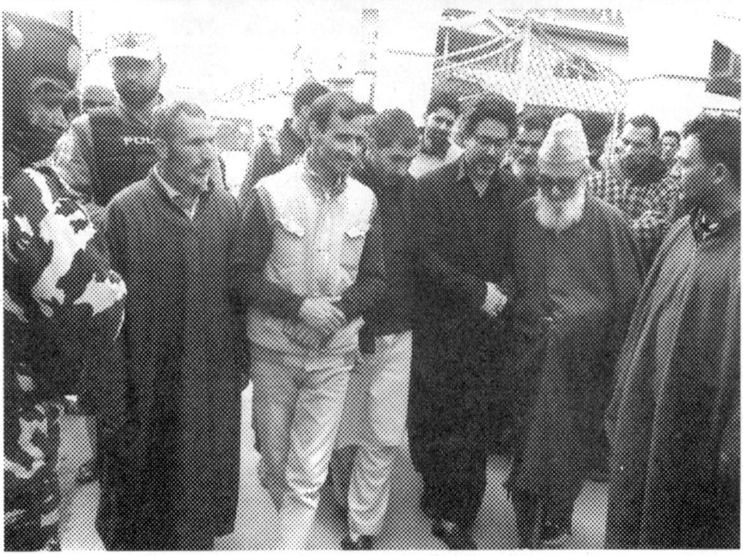

Campaigning for Lok Sabha elections in Srinagar

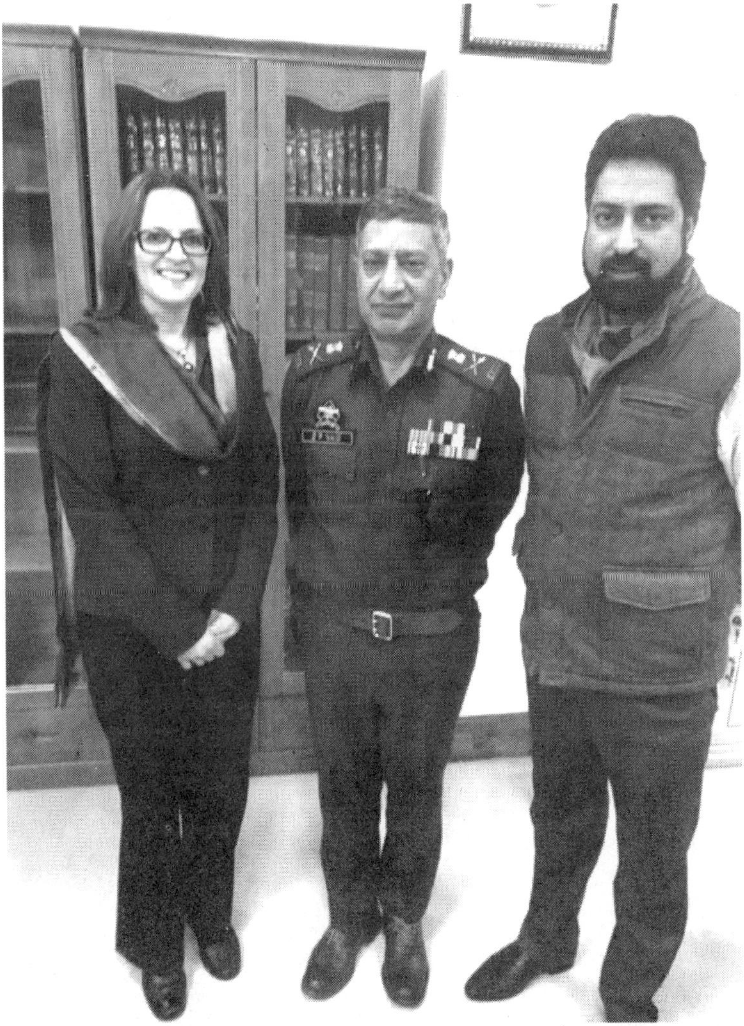

With USA deputy NSA Lisa Curtis and DGP J&K Dr S P Vaid in Srinagar

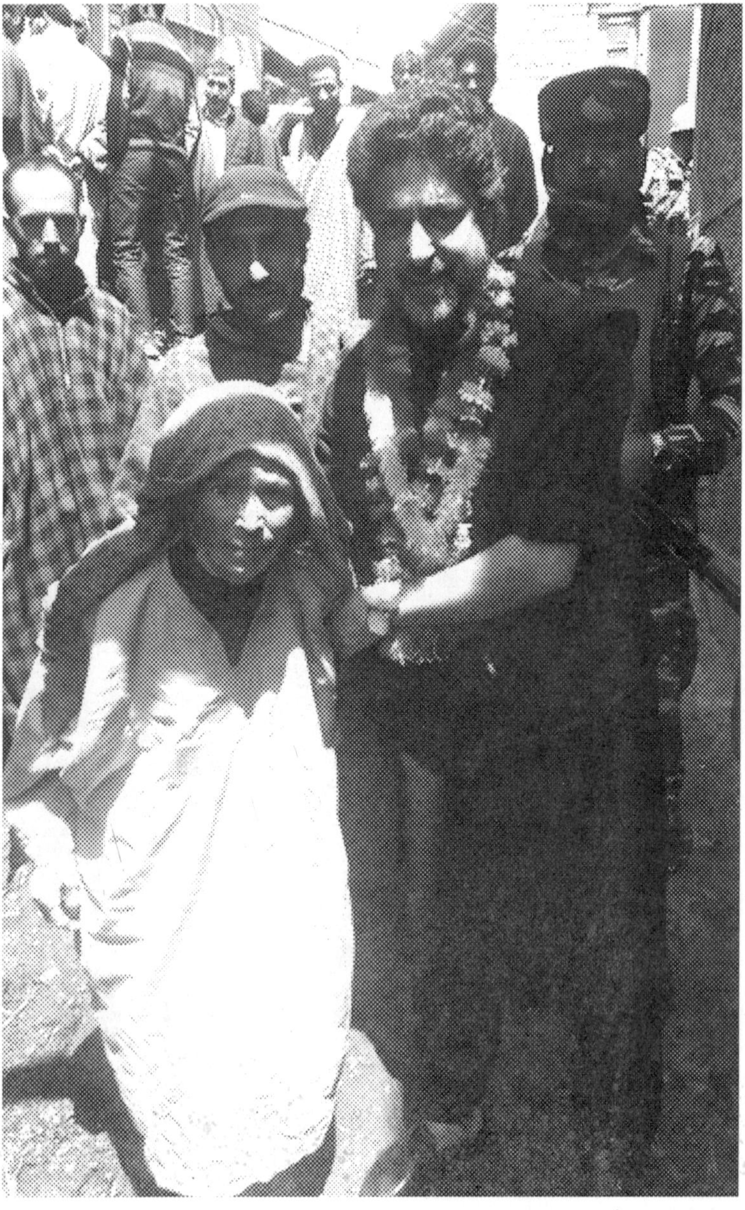

Getting blessing of an old woman voter during campaigning